China's Development Priorities

China's Development Priorities

Shahid Yusuf
Kaoru Nabeshima

THE WORLD BANK

ISBN-10: 0-8213-6509-6
ISBN-13: 978-0-8213-6509-0
eISBN-10: 0-8213-6510-X
eISBN-13: 978-0-8213-6510-6
DOI: 10.1596/978-0-8213-6509-0

Cover photo: Shanghai, China: ©2006 Getty Images

Library of Congress Cataloging-in-Publication Data

Yusuf, Shahid, 1949-
China's Development Priorities / Shahid Yusuf, Kaoru Nabeshima.
        P cm. – (Directions in development)
        Includes bibliographical references and index.
        ISBN-13: 978-0-8213-6509-0
ISBN-10: 0-8213-6609-6
1. China—Economic policy. 2. China—Economic conditions. I. Nabeshima, Kaoru. II.
        Title. III. Directions in development (Washington, D.C.)

        HC427.95.Y87 2006
        338.951—dc22   2006041016

Contents

Figures

Tables

Acknowledgments

This study was prepared in close consultation with China's National Development and Reform Commission (NDRC). We are deeply grateful to Yang Weimin and Xu Lin for their guidance. Throughout the preparation of this study, we cooperated with the U.K. Department for International Development (DFID), which generously supported the research and other activities financially and intellectually. We are especially indebted to Chris Athayde and Jillian Popkins.

We thank David Dollar, Homi Kharas, Yukon Huang, Bert Hofman, Deepak Bhattasali, and Sudarshan Gooptu for their support, encouragement, and comments throughout the preparation of this report.

The background notes commissioned for this report provided us with invaluable insights into China's development, future challenges, and policy options. The richness of the report owes much to the authors of the notes: Richard Bird, Era Dabla-Norris, Cindy Fan, Daniel Gunaratnam, Vernon Henderson, Patrick Honohan, Albert Park, Anthony Saich, Zmarak Shalizi, Edward Steinfeld, Kong-Yam Tan, John Taylor, Dana Weist, and Shiqing Xie.

We benefited from a number of written comments provided by external reviewers, participants of workshops held in Beijing, and colleagues at the World Bank. We thank the peer reviewers, Elizabeth Croll, Nicholas

Lardy, Vikram Nehru, and Dwight Perkins. Written comments were provided by Charles Abelman, Noureddine Berrah, Dan Biller, Shantayanan Devarajan, Tarhan Feyzioglu, Santiago Herrera, Emmanuel Jimenez, Louis Kuijs, Douglas Olson, David Scott, Graham Smith, Geoffrey Spencer, Xiaoqing Yu, Chunlin Zhang, and Jianping Zhao.

We also thank representatives from the NDRC, DFID, and the World Bank's China country team, who attended workshops held in Beijing and Washington, DC, and offered comments and suggestions.

We deeply appreciate the cheerful and dedicated assistance of Maribel Flewitt and Tristan Suratos in producing this manuscript and thank Jianqing Chen for her excellent support from the Beijing office, Tomoko Okano and Jue Sun for their valuable assistance with research, and Tianshu Chen for a careful translation of the study into Chinese.

About the Authors

Shahid Yusuf is a research manager of the Development Economics Research Group at the World Bank. He holds a Ph.D. in economics from Harvard University in Cambridge, Massachusetts. Dr. Yusuf is the team leader for the World Bank–Japan project on East Asia's Future Economy and was director of the *World Development Report 1999/2000: Entering the 21st Century*. Prior to that, he served the World Bank in several other capacities.

Dr. Yusuf has written extensively on development issues, with a special focus on East Asia. His publications include *China's Rural Development*, with Dwight Perkins (Johns Hopkins University Press 1984); *The Dynamics of Urban Growth in Three Chinese Cities*, with Weiping Wu (Oxford University Press 1997); *Rethinking the East Asian Miracle*, edited with Joseph Stiglitz (Oxford University Press 2001); *Can East Asia Compete? Innovation for Global Markets*, with Simon Evenett (Oxford University Press 2002); *Innovative East Asia: The Future of Growth*, with others (Oxford University Press 2003); *Global Production Networking and Technological Change in East Asia* and *Global Change and East Asian Policy Initiatives*, both edited with M. Anjum Altaf and Kaoru Nabeshima (Oxford University Press 2004); and *Under New Ownership: Privatizing China's State-Owned Enterprises* with Kaoru Nabeshima (Stanford

University Press 2005). He has also published widely in various academic journals.

Kaoru Nabeshima is an economist in the Development Economics Research Group at the World Bank. He holds a Ph.D. in economics from the University of California, Davis. Dr. Nabeshima is a team member for the World Bank–Japan project on East Asia's Future Economy and was a coauthor of *Innovative East Asia: The Future of Growth* (Oxford University Press 2003) and coeditor for *Global Production Networking and Technological Change in East Asia* and *Global Change and East Asian Policy Initiatives* (Oxford University Press 2004). His work on China includes *Under New Ownership: Privatizing China's State-Owned Enterprises* with Shahid Yusuf (Stanford University Press 2005). His research interests lie in the economic development of East Asia and the innovation capabilities of firms.

Acronyms and Abbreviations

AIDS	Acquired immunodeficiency syndrome
ASEAN	Association of South East Asian Nations
B2B	Business to business
CAGR	Compound aggregate growth rate
DFID	Department for International Development (U.K.)
FDI	Foreign direct investment
GDP	Gross domestic product
HIV	Human immunodeficiency virus
ICT	Information and communication technology
IT	Information technology
NDRC	National Development and Reform Commission
OECD	Organisation for Economic Co-operation and Development
PPP	Purchasing power parity
R&D	Research and development
SARS	Severe acute respiratory syndrome
TFP	Total factor productivity
TVE	Township and village enterprise
WTO	World Trade Organization

PART 1

On the Eve of the Eleventh Plan

CHAPTER 1

Introduction

During the Tenth Plan (2001–5), China's growth has been enviably rapid. Social indicators have continued improving, and in the aggregate poverty has inched downward. The prognosis for the Eleventh Plan (2006–10) is highly positive, but, at the same time, the plan needs to tackle emerging challenges that can affect the level and quality of growth: by some measures, inequality has worsened, the domestic resource and environmental costs of an expanding GDP are being felt, and the dependence on overseas suppliers for materials is rising at rates that cannot be sustained for long. If issues related to inequality and sustainability are neglected, China's growth could be jeopardized. If growth falters, it will become far harder to implement policies that will help to make a sustainable "all-around *xiaokang* society" into a reality during the next 15 years. This study seeks to answer three broad questions. What are the keys to rapid growth of greatest relevance to China during the Eleventh Plan period? What measures could contain and eventually reverse inequality? And what mix of policies could move China's economy in the direction of achieving sustainable growth while managing external dependence?

In the space of a little more than two decades, China has emerged as the world's fourth largest economy.[1] It now ranks third among trading nations, accounting for more than 6 percent of world trade; it is one of the leading industrial engines of the global economy.[2] But China's GDP per capita in 2005 was still a modest $1,730, and 416 million Chinese were subsisting on less than $2 a day. Moreover, the distribution of income is highly skewed, with urban income being three times the level of income in the rural sector. Thus average household income for the nation as a whole masks deep disparities between and within sectors and between the coastal and interior provinces. Incomes have grown rapidly, and income distribution has become more unequal during the past two decades. The first is responsible for substantial gains in household welfare and deep reductions in poverty. The second, while it reflects the workings of the market and of urbanization, could sow the seeds of social discontent and possibly slow the pace of growth.[3]

At the very start of China's reform drive in 1979, Deng Xiaoping envisioned a *xiaokang* society in which economic well being, if widely shared, would go hand in hand with social harmony.[4] While urging the Chinese people to make the country prosperous by "getting rich," Deng main-

---

1. Following the adjustment of China's GDP in December 2004, nominal GDP at the end of 2004 valued at the then prevailing exchange rate was $2.26 trillion. This makes China the fourth ranked economy, after Germany and ahead of the United Kingdom in 2005 when the GDP was estimated to have reached $2.7 trillion ("Too Fast" 2006). Using purchasing power parity (PPP) rates as the yardstick, China is now the second largest economy in the world ("Dragon and the Eagle" 2004).

2. In 1978 China ranked twenty-third in the world (Yao 2002). See also Eichengreen, Rhee, and Tong (2004). During 1995–2003, China's share of the growth in global GDP amounted to 23 percent

3. Rural-urban inequality and urban unemployment related to layoffs from the state sector are among the factors responsible for widespread, albeit localized, protests in the northeastern, central, and southwestern regions of China (Tanner 2004). The number of protests rose 6 percent between 2004 and 2005 to reach 87,000. This is four times the level in the mid-1990s ("In Face of Rural Unrest" 2006). Gilley (2004, pp. 104–5) wonders whether China might be moving from a state of "stable unrest" to the beginnings of a "metastatic crisis." See also "Cauldron Boils" (2005) as to whether such a crisis could arise from inequality and Banerjee and Duflo (2003) for an assessment of the econometric analysis underlying the relationship between growth and inequality. They find that a relationship is hard to discern, whether long term or short. Kanbur's (1996) review of this literature also reports inconclusive cross-country findings. Looking at this relationship from a different perspective, Ravallion and Chen (2004) find that faster growth rates do not lead to rising inequality and that, at least in agriculture during the 1980s, rapid growth was associated with falling inequality, although inequality was increasing in the urban sector.

4. The term *xiaokang* society refers to a well-off society in which all people can lead a fairly comfortable life. It was first used by Deng Xiaoping in the late 1970s. Deng defined

tained that *xiaokang* was the touchstone of a good society with Chinese characteristics. This theme was woven into the outline of the Eighth Five-Year Plan and strongly reiterated by Jiang Zemin at the Sixteenth Party Congress in November 2002. The Sixteenth National Congress of the Communist Party of China on November 17, 2002, proposed six qualitative targets: develop the economy, improve democracy, advance science and education, enrich culture, foster social harmony, and upgrade the texture of life of the people (Jiang 2002). Only one quantitative target—quadrupling of China's GDP of 2000 by 2020—was identified at that time. That is, by 2020, GDP per capita should reach $3,000, roughly equivalent to the average level for middle-income countries. Later, two additional quantitative targets were proposed to increase the ratio of urbanization to more than 50 percent and to decrease the ratio of rural employment to total employment from 50 percent in 2000 to 30 percent in 2020 ("Main Task of Economic Construction" 2002). In addition to material gain, China's leaders view building a *xiaokang* society as entailing improvement in the rule of law, civic life, the physical and natural environment, and the quality of leisure. Most important, the essence of *xiaokang* is the more equitable sharing of prosperity, rather than a mere improvement in growth prospects or social stability. A *xiaokang* society also has strong implications for China's current development strategy. According to Premier Wen Jiabao, it involves putting people first and promoting reform and innovation in accordance with the "five-balances": balancing urban and rural development, balancing development among regions, balancing economic and social development, balancing development between man and nature, and balancing domestic development with opening wider to the outside world (Wen 2004; see also "People Centered Development" 2004; UNDP 2004).

The Third Plenary Session of the Sixteenth Party Central Committee proposed guidelines for an "all-around *xiaokang* society," and at the Tenth National People's Congress, Premier Wen Jiabao indicated that combining growth with a more balanced distribution of income should be the guiding tenet for China's development (Nolan 2004). President Hu Jintao underscored this point in January 2006, when he pointed to the persistence of major contradictions and the need to narrow the gap between rural and urban incomes. China must also ensure that environmen-

---

xiaokang as achieving a target GDP per capita of $800 by 2000. Because of China's rapid economic growth, *xiaokang* was roughly achieved by the end of the twentieth century. Yet China's *xiaokang* "was still at lower level," "not all-inclusive," and "very uneven."

tal pollution and the resource costs of growth, already rising exponential-
ly, do not become unsupportable over the longer run and that the
dependence on overseas suppliers of food, energy, and other commodities
does not expose the economy to undue risk.

   Is the current development strategy compatible with rapid, balanced,
and sustainable long-term growth? If not, what policy initiatives should
be introduced during the Eleventh Plan announced by the Fifth Party
Plenum on October 11, 2005, and what outcomes should China be seeking (The 11th Five-Year Plan for National Economy and Social
Development" 2005)? These are the questions addressed in this study,
starting with a snapshot of China's development today and answers to the
questions regarding strategic imperatives and policy directions.

CHAPTER 2

Rising Incomes, Declining Poverty, Growing Inequality

Between 1979 and 2005, China's GDP per capita, denominated in U.S. dollars, rose fivefold, an achievement without parallel in the annals of development. It is all the more unusual when compared with the record of other transitioning economies, most of which embarked on major systemic reform around the late 1980s or early 1990s. The 25 transitioning economies in Eastern and Central Europe experienced sharp declines in output, and by 1999 only two had recovered the ground lost. In all the others, GDP was still below the levels reached in 1989 (Campos and Coricelli 2002, p. 802). According to a few indicators of economic performance, countries that embraced a "big bang" approach did somewhat better than ones that took a gradualist route (Balcerowicz 2003; Havrylyshyn 2004).[1] But even the most successful East European performers could not match China's economic prowess, for reasons having to do with China's economic structure (in particular, the dominance of agri-

---

1. Balcerowicz (2003) relies mainly on indicators of growth and distribution. Havrylyshyn (2004, p. 41) states that, even if one assumes that Hungary took a gradualist path, of "the nine rapid reformers, eight have done very well. Most of those that chose a more gradual path have had fewer economic benefits and surprisingly higher costs manifested in deterioration in indicators of well being and stalled progress in democratization."

culture), political stability enforced by a strong center, and the capacity to follow a flexible, decentralized path to the market.[2]

At the onset of reforms, more than 650 million Chinese were living on less than $1 a day. As incomes rose year after year, the incidence of poverty fell markedly in the first half of the 1980s, as a result of the strong performance of the agricultural sector, and then continued to decline at a slower pace through the late 1990s. After 1996, the number of people living below the $1 per day poverty line increased somewhat but then declined to 133 million in 2004, while the number living on less than $2 per day fell by more than 200 million. The poor are most numerous in the rural parts of the central and western provinces (World Bank 2003a).[3] Urban poverty is lower, and between 4.7 and 6.5 percent of the urban population falls below the poverty line, pegged at an annual income of Y2,310 (Taylor 2004a).[4] Table 2.1 shows the downward movement of

Table 2.1. China's Poverty Headcount, 1990–2004
millions of persons

Year	Population	Population living on less than $1 a day	Population living on less than $2 a day
1990	1,143	360.6	799.6
1993	1,185	343.9	769.8
1996	1,224	200.8	631.6
1998	1,248	201.2	620.8
1999	1,258	218.4	623.6
2000	1,267	194.8	567.4
2001	1,276	183.0	529.6
2002	1,285	167.4	495.2
2003	1,292	152.2	460.7
2004	1,300	133.2	415.7

Source: World Bank 2005b.

---

2. Sachs and Woo (1997) note the significance of a large agricultural sector, while others refer to the degree of decentralization, the authority and power of the central government, and a gradualist approach that avoided a sudden unraveling of input-output (I-O) relationships, such as that which caused "disorganization" in East Europe (Blanchard and Kremer 1997).

3. In 2000 almost 14 percent of rural households had incomes of less than $1 per day. The incidence of poverty was highest in Gansu, Guizhou, Ningxia, Qinghai, Shanxi, and Yunnan. Increasingly, many of the poor are minorities, are living in remote areas where the quality of land is poor, do not have access to education or markets, are less likely to participate in off-farm employment, and face acute shortages of water (Taylor 2004a).

4. The ranks of the urban poor are filled by the elderly, the disabled, some migrants, and farmers from urban counties who have been displaced from their land and forced into low-paid jobs (Taylor 2004a).

Table 2.2. Inequality Indexes in China, 1981–2004

| Year | Gini index | | | Income per capita (current prices in RMB) | | Ratio of urban to rural income per capita |
	National[b]	Rural	Urban	Rural	Urban	
1981	30.95	24.73	18.46	223.4	500.4	2.24
1985	29.39	27.12	17.08	397.6	739.1	1.86
1987	33.73	29.45	17.13	462.6	1,002.1	2.17
1991	37.06	30.57	24.78	708.6	1,700.6	2.40
1992	39.01	32.03	24.17	784.0	2,026.6	2.58
1993	41.95	32.13	28.47	921.6	2,577.4	2.80
1994	43.31	34.00	29.22	1,221.0	3,496.2	2.86
1995	41.50	33.98	28.27	1,557.7	4,283.0	2.75
1996	39.75	33.62	29.09	1,926.1	4,838.9	2.51
1997	39.78	33.12	29.35	2,090.0	5,160.3	2.47
1998	40.33	33.07	29.94	2,162.0	5,425.1	2.51
1999	41.61	35.39	31.55	2,210.0	5,854.0	2.65
2001	44.73	36.33	33.32	2,366.4	6,859.6	2.90
2002	—	—	—	2,475.6	7,702.8	3.11
2003	46.00[b]	—	—	2,622.2	8,472.2	3.23
2004	—	—	—	2,936.4	9,421.6	3.21

Source: National Bureau of Statistics of China, *China Statistical Abstract*, 2003; World Bank, *PovcalNet*, at http://research.worldbank.org/PovcalNet/jsp/index.jsp.
— Not available.
a. Based on data provided by Shaohua Chen, World Bank.
b. Estimated.

poverty over the decade from 1990 to 2001. Clearly poverty is on the retreat, but huge numbers of people still lead a precarious existence and remain vulnerable to poverty.

In the late 1970s China was one of the most egalitarian societies in the world. The nationwide Gini coefficient was 0.33 (it is now 0.46), although the ratio of rural to urban income was 1:2.2 (Riskin 1987; World Bank 2005a).[5] This was achieved mainly through the system of centralized planning, which maintained tight control over urban wages, the earnings of farm households, and prices. The piecemeal dismantling of controls on prices, production, and the movement of people and the emergence of a robust market economy with a thriving private sector have made incomes—and wealth—less equal. Such a tendency was almost inevitable. Surprising, however, is the speed with which the distribution of income has diverged. Table 2.2 shows how far and how fast China has moved away from a state of relative equality as measured by the Gini coefficient.[6] If urban nonincome benefits are included (such as material income and subsidies), the ratio of urban to rural income was 1:3.6 in 2000 (Fan 2004b). In the majority of countries around the world, urban incomes are typically no more than twice the level of rural income (Tan 2004). Moreover, income disparities within both rural and urban areas have risen since the early 1990s. Among lower-middle-income countries, distribution in China is now among the most unequal.

The number of people living in poverty and the intersectoral disparities in income suggest that China is well short of its goal of a *xiaokang* society. Moreover, the persistence of these income differentials, in conjunction with the pressures generated by structural changes, could begin to erode national cohesion and generate tensions within and among provinces.[7] The seriousness of the situation will be further modulated by

5. Riskin (1987) maintains that the ratio was probably closer to between 1:2.5 and 1:3 and cites other estimates suggesting that it could have been as high as 1:5.9 if urban subsidies are factored in. This suggests that, compared with today, income differentials in the late 1970s were as wide.

6. Kanbur and Zhang (2001) associate inequality in China with the strategy to develop and disperse heavy industry—the earlier centralized approach—and the more recent opening up of the economy, which favored the coastal areas. Within-province inequality between rural and urban areas now contributes significantly to overall inequality (OECD 2005a). However, Keng (2005) finds that 60 percent of income inequality in China is the result of interprovincial disparities, while only 40 percent comes from intraprovincial sources.

7. Ravallion (2004) points to another problem associated with inequality. He indicates that, for any given rate of GDP growth, the more unequal the income distribution, the lower the gains accruing to the lowest-income deciles.

ongoing developments in the rural and urban sectors. The agricultural sector is subject to tightening constraints arising from water stress in the northern areas and the loss of arable land to urbanization and desertification.[8] As a result, wheat production in the north and northeast has been declining, well before China's accession to the World Trade Organization (WTO). How these developments will impinge on farm incomes will depend on the scope for moving into horticultural products and the growth of market opportunities for such products within China and overseas. Livestock production also offers opportunities. As figure 2.1 shows, farmers are compensating for falling wheat output by shifting into other crops, as reflected in rising primary production.

Rural township and village industries are also being rationalized as a result of domestic market integration, which is forcing many small, uncompetitive firms to exit and others to form enterprise groups, improve product standards, and reduce steep debt burdens (Smyth,

Figure 2.1: Wheat Production and Primary Output in China, 1990–2004

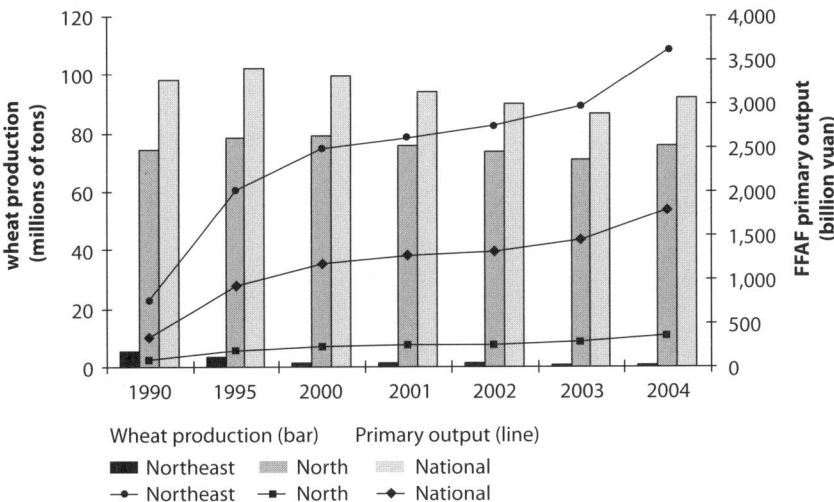

Wheat production (bar)   Primary output (line)
■ Northeast   ▨ North   ▨ National
◆ Northeast   ■ North   ◆ National

Source: National Bureau of Statistics of China, *China Statistical Yearbook*, 1991, 1996, 2001–5.

---

8. Close to 2.5 million square kilometers of land are now classified as desert (25 percent of China's land area), and 3,400 square kilometers are being added each year ("Desertification Damage" 2002). By one estimate, 6.5 million hectares of prime agricultural land have been lost to urbanization since the mid-1980s.

Wang, and Kiang 2002).[9] Furthermore, a scarcity of capital for potential new entrants, exacerbated by financial market imperfections, has slowed the entry of new firms in rural areas. Nevertheless, employment in township and village enterprises (TVEs) is recovering and in 2004 just exceeded the 1996 peak (see table 2.3);[10] if private enterprises are included, rural employment is now higher than in the mid-1990s. However, rural industry is unlikely to be a leading sector over the medium and longer term. Industry will tend to gravitate toward urban and periurban locations to reap the benefits of scale and agglomeration economies. In the face of these developments, both of which will progressively reduce agricultural and rural employment, the only real long-term solution is for people to move to the cities. Urbanization continues to be the worldwide trend as well: 39 percent of the world population was urbanized in 1980 (as well as 39 percent of the population in middle-income countries), compared with 48 percent in 2002 (53 percent in middle-income countries). But

Table 2.3. Employment in Township and Village Enterprises and Private Enterprises in Rural Areas of China, 1985–2004

thousands of persons

Year	Township and village enterprises	Private enterprises
1985	69,790	—
1990	92,650	1,130
1995	128,620	4,710
1996	135,080	5,510
1997	130,500	6,000
1998	125,370	7,370
1999	127,040	9,690
2000	128,200	11,390
2001	130,860	11,870
2002	132,880	14,110
2003	135,730	17,540
2004	138,660	20,240

Source: National Bureau of Statistics of China, *China Statistical Abstract,* various years.
— Not available.

---

9. Many township and village enterprises have been privatized or quasi-privatized.
10. TVEs were a major source of China's growth through the mid-1990s, when dispersed development in rural areas was favored over urban-industrial growth (Dacosta and Carroll 2001). Their proliferation was also associated with regional inequality, as they were less numerous and less productive in the inland areas (Ito 2002). The contribution of TVEs to growth and employment has diminished since the checks on urbanization were eased.

absorbing migrants into the urban economy could become problematic in certain areas. Although urban job growth has been robust on average, especially in the service industries and construction, unemployment has risen as troubled state-owned enterprises have laid off workers. Many of these workers have been unable to secure alternative employment in spite of some effort at retaining state-owned enterprises and local authorities. Where displaced and unemployed workers have difficulty obtaining pension benefits from their employer or these prove insufficient even for bare necessities, they are subject to considerable hardship and have increasingly engaged in public protests in order to seek redress. In the context of rapid growth, the ability of policy actions to ease this transition will depend on urbanization strategies and the division of responsibilities for managing and financing this process among different levels of government.

Geographic Concentration of Development and the Sources of Growth

The scale and pattern of urbanization in China are unusual for a country at China's level of income. In 2005, 43 percent of the population resided in urban areas (see table 2.4). This is because, since the 1950s, China has controlled the movement of population and held down the cost to the state of financing the housing and benefits of urban workers, most of whom enjoy lifetime employment (Murphey 1980; Putterman and Dong 2000). There are relatively few mega cities, and many of China's cities are suboptimal in scale (Henderson 2004b).[11] In 1998 just nine metropolitan areas had populations exceeding 3 million, while another 125 had popu-

Table 2.4. Urban Population in China, 1995–2004

Year	Percent of total population	Number of persons (millions)
1995	29.0	352.0
2000	36.2	459.0
2005	43.0	559.0

Source: National Bureau of Statistics of China, *China Statistical Yearbook,* 2005.

---

11. Henderson (2004b) calculates that most cities at the prefectural level are below optimal size, whereas cities at the provincial level are either at or somewhat above their optimal size.

lations between 1 million and 3 million.[12] This is very low relative to countries of comparable size and income. Moreover, the Gini coefficient for accumulated share of the population in cities ranked from the smallest to the largest was 0.43 in 2000 compared with 0.56 for the world as a whole and 0.65 for Brazil, 0.60 for Indonesia and Mexico, 0.58 for India, and 0.54 for the United States. In other words, China's urban populace is dispersed to a far greater degree among the smaller cities (Fujita and others 2004).

Since the 1980s, however, China is slowly coming to resemble other countries in the geographic distribution of the population, economic activity, and sectoral sources of growth. The major impetus for growth comes from the urban-industrial sector, which is absorbing migrants leaving the rural areas; the fastest-growing industries are located mostly in China's major coastal cities and occasionally along the main inland waterways. Close to 70 percent of the increase in the urban population is the result of in-migration.[13] Among China's provinces and cities with provincial status, the highest in-migration has been recorded by Guangdong, Shandong, Shanghai, Jiangsu, Beijing, and Jiangsu, in that order. As a percentage of the local population, Shanghai and Beijing have attracted the most migrants (Johnson 2003). Currently, 493 million people live in the coastal provinces, and 430 million live in the central region. The normal process of development, mediated by the market, would most likely lead to increasing concentration of people in cities along the eastern seaboard (see figure 2.2). How China will shape these urbanization trends will determine much of the productivity and resource intensity of the economy and the amount of infrastructure needed to sustain growth. China's current policy of promoting secondary and small cities may not be optimal in that respect.

So long as the major metropolitan regions can accommodate population growth and keep congestion and the costs of pollution in check, this policy can produce efficient economic outcomes as well as rising urban employment.[14] In fact, the increasing concentration of the urban population is being paralleled by a concentration of manufacturing, reflected in

---

12. The 10 largest cities in China accounted for just 19 percent of the urban population, compared with 37 percent in the United States (DFID 2004).
13. This is an upper bound because some of the increase can be traced to the reclassification of rural counties contiguous to cities (Park 2004).
14. In Hangzhou, for instance, congestion, air pollution from vehicles, and a shortage of public spaces and housing are all worsening in spite of investment in infrastructure, indicating that sustaining livability and efficiency might well prove to be difficult (Wei and Li 2002).

Figure 2.2: Population Distribution in China, by Regions, 1985–2004

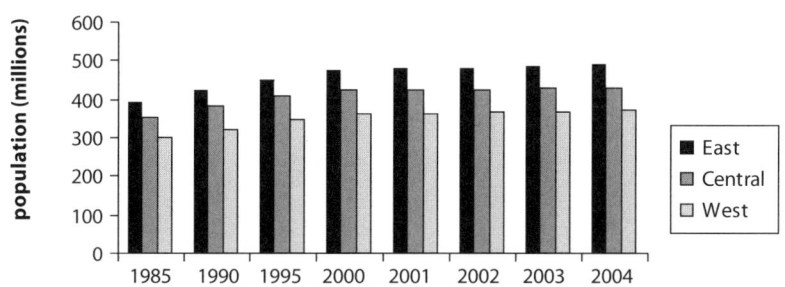

East: Beijing, Fujian Guangdong, Hainan, Hebei, Hunan, Jiangsu, Liaoning, Shangdong, Shanghai, Tianjin, and Zhejiang
Central: Anhui, Heilongjiang, Henan, Hubei, Jiangxi, Jilin, and Shanxi
West: Chongqing, Gansu, Guangxi, Guizhou, Inner Mongolia, Ningxia, Qinghai, Shaanxi, Sichuan, Tibet, Xinjiang, and Yunnan.

Source: China Statistical Yearbook (various issues)

rising Gini coefficients for industry during 1980–95, with an apparent focus on urban centers in a few coastal provinces. Table 2.5 shows a steady upward shift in the Gini coefficient for industry during 1980–95. This is reinforced by table 2.6, which highlights the presence of key industries, such as the producers of computers, autos, white goods, and brown goods in the east coast provinces. The principal attractors are Guangdong, Jiangsu, and Shanghai. Together, the three generated 28 percent of China's GDP in 2004, produced 59 percent of exports in 2004, and absorbed 47 percent of foreign direct investment (FDI) in 2004 (see table 2.7).

Large cities, which have a diversified industrial base, offer agglomeration economies, and their economic performance as well as employment rates tend to be relatively stable (Scott and Storper 2003).[15] Cities such as Beijing, Guangzhou, Hangzhou, Shanghai, Suzhou, and Wuhan are the industrial pacesetters and the leaders in industrial technology. In 1995 coastal provinces filed 65 percent of all patent applications. Beijing, Guangdong, Jiangsu, Liaoning, Shandong, and Zhejiang accounted for 50 percent of domestic patent applications,[16] while patent applications from

15. All the major metropolitan areas in China are highly diversified. To give one example, Ningbo, a medium-size city in Zhejiang, has producers in 68 of 70 three-digit manufacturing categories, and this is also true, of course, for all the larger metropolitan areas (Fujita and others 2004).
16. In 2004, 6.6 percent of invention patents filed by domestic residents were from Beijing, and 7.3 percent were from Shanghai, up from 4 percent in 1995 ("State Intellectual Property Office of China" 2005).

Table 2.5. Industrial Concentration (Gini) and Regions with the Highest and the Second Highest Industrial Shares, 1980, 1985, and 1995

	1980		1985		1995	
Industry	Gini	Top-two regions	Gini	Top two regions	Gini	Top two regions
Cultural, educational, and sports goods	0.712	SH,BJ	0.696	SH,GD	0.756	GD,JS
Electronic and communications equipment	0.593	SH,JS	0.584	JS,SH	0.701	GD,JS
Garments and other fiber products	0.446	SH,JS	0.473	SH,JS	0.692	GD,JS
Chemical fibers	0.720	SH,JS	0.667	SH,JS	0.684	JS,SH
Electric equipment and machinery	0.509	SH,LN	0.525	SH,JS	0.644	GD,JS
Textiles	0.555	SH,JS	0.554	JS,SH	0.641	JS,ZJ
Plastic products	0.513	JS,SH	0.526	JS,ZJ	0.630	GD,JS
Instruments, meters, cultural, and office machinery	0.554	SH,JS	0.549	SH,JS	0.629	GD,SH
Metal products	0.477	SH,JS	0.479	SH,JS	0.596	JS,GD
Furniture	0.388	GD,SD	0.414	GD,JS	0.547	GD,SD
Rubber products	0.467	SH,SD	0.447	SH,SD	0.536	SD,SH
Transport equipment	0.477	LN,HUB	0.473	HUB,LN	0.534	SH,JS

Source: Wen Mei 2004b.

Note: Regions are abbreviated in this table as follows: Beijing, BJ; Guangdong, GD; Hubei, HUB; Jiangsu, JS; Liaoning, LN; Shandong, SD; Shanghai, SH; and Zhejiang, ZH.

Table 2.6. Key Industries in China, by Region, Five-Year Averages, 1999–2003
percent

Region	Steel	Paper and board	Beer	Washing machines	Color television	Motor vehicles	Computers
Northeast	27.7	10.0	14.4	4.3	1.9	11.3	35.3
North	13.3	4.7	16.7	1.2	10.2	24.5	7.6
Middle coast	31.5	45.3	37.9	71.0	29.2	30.6	29.0
South coast	16.1	29.1	19.6	19.4	41.8	19.6	26.9
Southwest	8.3	4.2	7.0	1.8	15.2	13.1	0.5
Far west	3.1	6.6	4.3	2.4	1.8	0.9	0.6

Source: "China: A Five-Year Outlook" 2004.

Table 2.7. Shares of Guangdong, Jiangsu, and Shanghai in GDP, Exports, and FDI, 2004
percent

Province	GDP	Exports	FDI[a]
Shanghai	5.44	12.39	10.79
Jiangsu	11.25	14.75	20.03
Guangdong	11.72	32.29	16.52
Total	28.41	59.42	47.34

Source: National Bureau of Statistics of China, *China Statistical Yearbook,* 2005.
a. Shanghai Municipal Statistical Bureau 2006; Jiangsu Municipal Statistics Bureau 2005; *East Asia Economic Review,* January 17, 2005, www.e-economic.com/info/1009-1.htm; Department of Foreign Trade and Economic Cooperation of Guangdong http://www.gddoftec.gov.cn/gdgl/a1.html.

the central and western regions were 23 and 12 percent, respectively (Cheung and Lin 2004). This disparity widened in 2000, with the share of patent applications from the coastal region increasing to 72 percent and those from the central and western regions falling to 18 and 10 percent, respectively (Cheung and Lin 2004). The coastal region has also been at the forefront of the reform drive. To sustain this momentum, the coastal areas—and other provinces that are seeking to catch up—will need to take initiatives in three policy areas during the Eleventh Plan and well into the future.[17]

The first policy area encompasses the business environment. Growing urban centers that drive economic performance and serve as the primary locus of innovations depend on the quality of urban management, urban infrastructure, and the efficiency of urban markets to attract and retain jobs. When cities create an abundance of jobs with high value added, the

17. Inland provinces such as Sichuan are achieving greater success in attracting industrial investment and stimulating high-tech development around Chengdu ("Go West" 2005).

transfer of labor out of the agricultural sector raises productivity and, through it, growth. Many factors contribute to urban dynamism, such as the entry and growth of firms that provide jobs, which in turn is related to the quality of municipal services and the effectiveness of the regulatory institutions. These affect the production and transaction costs of firms and hence their competitiveness. With Chinese cities vying with each other and also with other major East Asian urban regions for industrial capital, municipalities must streamline regulations and offer world-class infrastructure facilities.

The productivity and innovativeness of businesses operating in an urban center are a second area that demands attention. This is linked to the national innovation system, but it is equally a function of the use of information technology (IT) and FDI, among others. Ease of entry and exit of firms, access to risk capital, and economic openness are all important in this regard. The evidence overwhelmingly suggests that large productivity gains can be realized in the manufacturing industries producing IT-related equipment and the principal users of IT such as wholesale, retail, financial, legal, and logistical services (Gordon 2004; McKinsey Global Institute 2001; Solow 2001).

At the firm level, companies that invest in IT usually employ relatively skilled workers, have a higher level of productivity, tend to enlarge their market share, and spend more on research and development (R&D). Indeed, as pointed out in a recent report (OECD 2004b, p. 86), "Computer networks allow a firm to outsource certain activities to work closer with customers and suppliers and to better integrate activities through the value chain. . . . Average labor productivity is higher in plants with networks . . . by about 5 percent. . . . The impact of direct business operations networks, such as production and logistic control systems, on productivity is much clearer than that of back office supporting systems, such as human resource management and management planning systems." Among Chinese firms, IT use is highest in joint ventures and in firms that are linked to international production networks and invest most heavily in IT, highlighting the significance of FDI (Yusuf and Evenett 2002).

Embodied technological change and technological spillovers also contribute to gains in productivity as a result of FDI. China is the largest recipient of FDI inflows among developing countries, receiving one-quarter of the total for the past decade or 9.9 percent of FDI worldwide (Zhao 2005). In 2005 FDI inflow was $60.3 billion,[18] exceeding the projection

---

18. *Jinhua Times*, January 26, 2006, http://news.soufun.com/2006-01-26/627369.htm.

of $54 billion; of this, close to 70 percent flowed into industry (Liu and Wang 2003).[19] In 2004 three-quarters of FDI was in industry; of this, 71 percent went into manufacturing. This represents 11 percent of total investment, but a higher share of investment in the coastal region, which attracted 90 percent of FDI ("International: Developing World" 2004; Zhao 2005). Moreover, China's stock of FDI to GDP climbed from 1 percent in 1986 to 34 percent in 2004 ("Faintly Declining Investment" 2005).

Productivity and innovativeness are negatively influenced by the presence of numerous state-owned enterprises that monopolize a significant share of the financing available through the public banking system (Honohan 2004). State-owned enterprises introduce market distortions that reduce the number of new entrants (which often serve as the vehicle for innovation) and impede the growth of promising incumbent firms. Efforts by local governments to protect state-owned enterprises have tended to interfere with the integration of the national market for products, further constraining the growth and innovativeness of firms. A more integrated national market could lead to a greater geographic coalescence of industrial activity. A concentration of economic power in a small number of sprawling metropolitan regions has its merits. However, in the absence of greater labor productivity, it could exacerbate the economic differences between the coastal region and other parts of China.

The labor market in China is fragmented because of restrictions on permanent migration to urban centers, a third issue. As a result, the marginal return to labor in 2001 was Y365 in agriculture, while it was Y11,884 in urban industry, Y4,672 in rural nonfarm employment, and Y2,009 in urban services, indicating large distortions in the labor market, especially between agriculture and urban industry. This disparity in the labor productivity ratio increased from 11.4 in 1978 to 34 in 2001 (Tan 2004). Had this surplus labor been employed in the nonagricultural sector, it would have added output equal to Y2.4 trillion, about one third of GDP in 1997 (Chen 2001).[20]

---

19. For the inflow of FDI in 2004, see "UN Reports Upsurge" 2005; for the estimates, see "International: Developing World" 2004; Liu and Wang 2003. Hong Kong (China) received an additional $13 billion of FDI in 2003 ("International: Developing World" 2004).

20. Distortions in the financial markets are striking. For one, the variation in the marginal product of capital, which had declined from 0.23 in 1978 to 0.16 in 1991, rose to 0.35 by 2001. Another indicator of market distortions is the difference in the capital-labor ratio across the four regions: in 2001 the ratio of 173.2 in the coastal region was 2.6 times the ratio of 65.9 in the western region, compared with 25.9 and 24.4, respectively, in 1978.

As restrictions imposed by the *hukou* (registered permanent residence) system have weakened, the flow of migrants to cities has risen.[21] As a result, access to social services by migrants and their families will become an increasingly binding constraint on labor mobility. Most migrants are being drawn to coastal cities by the prospects of earning higher incomes, with the larger urban centers topping the list of destinations. Migration provides China's cities with a youthful, motivated, and entrepreneurial workforce, results in a large productivity bonus, supports industrial advance, and keeps downward pressure on wages.[22] Migration also ameliorates rural hardship because it provides an outlet for unemployed or underemployed rural workers; once migrants have found urban jobs, they become a source of remittances to rural households, which now account for close to half of household incomes in some provinces (Fan 2004b).[23] The agricultural labor surplus in 2001 was estimated at between 150 million to 200 million (Cai 2001; Cao 2001; Wang 2001; Zhang and Lin 2000), with an additional 13 million persons projected to join this pool between 2001 and 2010 (Qiu 2001). According to the 2000 census, more than 10 percent of the population is on the move, almost 124 million people (Fan 2004b).[24] The census conducted in 2002 estimated that the floating population was close to 144 million ("1.46 Billion" 2004). Of these migrants, 41 percent were rural-urban, 37 percent were urban-urban, and 18 percent were rural-rural migrants (Cai and Wang 2003).[25]

---

21. Barriers to labor mobility from the enforcement of the *hukou* and the associated restrictions on access to housing and social services to migrants, while diminishing, continue to divide the labor market. By 2001 the labor productivity ratio of urban industry, urban services, and rural nonfarm labor to that of agriculture in China was an astonishing four to 10 times that in other countries (Indonesia, Japan, Korea, Malaysia, the Philippines, and United States) and in Taiwan (China).
22. Bloom and Williamson (1997) ascribe between 1.4 and 1.9 percent of the annual growth in GDP in East Asia between 1965 and 1990 to demographics, which affected labor force growth, age structure, domestic savings, and domestic investment. In 2005, 71 percent of China's population was between the ages of 15 and 64 years.
23. Typically remittances by migrant workers raise household incomes by 9 to 13 percent, although the amount of remittance depends on the needs of other family members and can be higher in provinces where household incomes are low (Du, Park, and Wang 2005).
24. According to the 1990 census, there were 35 million migrants. However, the definition of migrants changed between the 1990 and 2000 census. The 2000 census considers as migrants those who changed their location at the subcounty level for at least six months, whereas the 1990 census considers as migrants those who changed county-level locations for more than one year (Fan 2004b).
25. Two-thirds of migrants are male (average age of 28) and typically have a junior high school–level education. This is lower than that of the average urban resident (Fan

However, migration is fraught with problems that require the attention of policy makers. It can drain the countryside of the better educated[26] and most enterprising young male workers, leading to an aging and "feminization" of the agricultural labor force.[27] Migration also creates problems in the cities that are the preferred destinations. Migrants need jobs, low-cost housing, health care, and schooling for their children. Without these, they are at risk of descending into poverty.[28] The U.K. Department for International Development (DFID 2004), citing Meng, Li, and Eggleston (2004), notes that income poverty among urban migrants rose from 2 to 4 percent and higher between 1986 and 2000, while consumption poverty doubled from 5 to 10 percent. In 31 of 50 cities surveyed by the Asia Development Bank (ADB 2004), migrants were, on average, less well off than other urban residents, but, in at least a third of the cities covered, the poverty rate was higher among the local population than among migrants.[29]

These interlaced policy issues are by no means the only ones that will challenge China's policy makers as they grapple with some of the institutional, sectoral, and spatial dimensions of economic growth. However, in view of the importance that policy makers are attaching to balance, these dimensions deserve priority during the course of the Eleventh Plan and, most likely, well beyond.

Containing the Resource Intensity of Development

Sustainable development in the Chinese context has many parts. Of these, energy use, water use, and their environmental effects are the three most important.[30]

2004b), because enterprises commonly hire only those who have finished at least junior high school (Park 2004). Often, the husband pursues migrant work, while the wife stays in the village to take care of the farm.

26. Research on rural Mexico suggests that the lure of urban opportunities spurs rural youth to acquire more education (Boucher, Stark, and Taylor 2005).

27. Because of this, women account for more than 50 percent of labor in the primary industry (Taylor 2004a). Only 2.4 percent of women remaining on farms have high school degrees as opposed to 5.6 percent of men; the illiteracy rate is 22 percent for women and 12 percent for men (Taylor 2004a).

28. On the other social issues related to migration, see Bielke (2004); Chan (1998); "China Eases Rules" (2001); Ma (2001); Zhang (2001).

29. Based on the income available to migrants after remittances, the National Bureau of Statistics of China estimates that 3 million migrants are living in poverty (Taylor 2004a).

30. The degradation of China's fragile land areas is a fourth concern (FAS 2003; Smil 1984, 2004), although a study of China's soil quality from the 1930s through the 1980s ques-

Energy

The world's most populous country and fastest-growing economy has resource requirements that are beginning to rival those of Japan and the United States. Directly comparing energy intensity per dollar of GDP between countries is a complex undertaking. Nominal GDP overstates China's energy intensity. For this reason, a PPP measure of GDP is sometimes preferred, which brings China's energy intensity closer to the world average. In kilograms of energy use per dollar of PPP-adjusted GDP in 2003, China used 0.23 kilograms, approximately the same as the United States and Indonesia and a little less than Korea (0.24) and Malaysia (0.25).[31]

The reality is probably in between these two measures. A better comparison is energy consumption per unit of production for particular industries or products. Eleven major industrial sectors—coal, petroleum, refining, power, steel, nonferrous metal, building materials, chemicals, light industry, textiles, and railways and transportation—use about 80 percent of the energy consumed in industry and transportation. Analysis of energy inputs reveals that the average value of energy consumption for 13 products in these industries was higher than international levels of developed countries by 6 to 36 percent in 2000—for example, among the highest were steel, 124 percent; cement, 145 percent; power generation, 125 percent; and fuel use in trucks, 123 percent.

China has traditionally depended on coal, which still supplies 67 percent of the primary energy consumed, as against the world average of 24 percent ("China: High Oil Prices" 2005). However, higher transport demand and efforts to diversify the mix of fuels have increased the use of petroleum. China's consumption of oil more than doubled between 1992 and 2004, from 133 million tons to 292 million tons, and China was the world's second largest consumer in 2005 ("China: High Oil Prices" 2005). China accounted for 41 percent of the growth in world demand for oil in 2003 and for a third over the past 10 years (Cornelius and Story 2005; "World Reserves of Oil" 2004). Consumption in 2005 averaged an esti-

---

tions this. Lindert suggests that, on average, China has suffered no "net loss of soil endowment . . . Soil nutrients that have declined are those that are replaceable at the margin by quick-release fertilizers" (Lindert 1999, p. 702). Moreover, "The average quality of China's cultivated soils rose modestly from the 1950s to the 1980s" (Lindert 1999, p. 723).

31. By comparison, energy use was 0.15 kilogram in Japan and in Western Europe (World Bank 2005b).

Table 2.8. Output and Consumption of Oil and Gas in China, 1992–2004

Year	Oil (million tons)		Gas (billion cubic meters)	
	Production	Consumption	Production	Consumption
1992	142.0	133.0	15.1	15.1
1995	149.5	169.5	17.6	17.7
1999	160.5	221.0	24.3	21.4
2000	162.5	249.5	27.2	24.5
2001	165.5	251.5	30.3	27.8
2002	167.5	269.0	31.9	29.6
2003	170.0	299.0	34.4	32.8
2004	174.5	308.6	40.8	39.0

Source: BP 2005.

Note: The figures for oil were converted using 1 barrel per day = 50 tons per year.

mated 6.2 million barrels a day, with imports supplying nearly 40 percent (see table 2.8).

Assuming that GDP increases 7–8 percent a year, the annual demand for oil could approach 500 million tons by 2010, while domestic production is unlikely to exceed 180 million tons ("China: A Five-Year Outlook" 2004). In comparison, oil consumption in Japan is currently 300 million tons ("China: Surging Oil" 2004). Much will depend on the increase in the number of passenger vehicles, which numbered 27 million in 2004, with the stock rising more than 4 million a year. Vehicles could account for close to half of all oil consumption within a decade.

Income elasticity of urban energy use is about 0.7, meaning that a 10 percent increase in income will lead to a 7 percent increase in demand for energy (Henderson 2004b). By comparison, the overall elasticity of energy consumption is 0.34 (Zhang 2003). The higher urban elasticity arises from the acquisition of electronic appliances by urban households. For instance, since 1985 in urban areas, ownership of refrigerators has increased from 7 to 75 percent, ownership of televisions has increased from 17 to 86 percent, and the use of air conditioning units has risen steeply. As a result, electricity consumption has risen dramatically, with income elasticity of 1.8 in 2003 (Steinfeld 2004b).[32] In cities such as Beijing, the use of air conditioning accounts for as much as 40 percent of the energy used during the summertime peak, exacerbating an already tight supply of power ("Power Shortage Sees" 2004). The quality of insu-

---

32. By comparison, in 2000, 49 percent of rural households owned a color television, 29 percent owned a washing machine, and only 1.3 percent owned a refrigerator (Rong and Yao 2003).

lation in Chinese housing is grossly inefficient, and space heating or cooling consumes between 50 and 100 percent more energy than in developed countries in similar climatic zones (Steinfeld 2004b). Less than 5 percent of new housing units meet energy conservation standards ("Energy Conservation" 2004). Thus the scope for conserving energy is substantial.

Water

Although China has the fifth largest natural flow of water in the world, at 2.8 trillion cubic meters a year in 2000, this constitutes only 2,219 cubic meters per person, just one fourth of the world average of 8,649 cubic meters per person.[33] Since the natural flow of water does not change significantly (except for the yearly fluctuation linked to total rainfall) and the population is growing, the availability of water per capita is declining.[34] Water shortage in 2000 was calculated at close to 30 billion cubic meters for the entire country and is expected to reach 57 billion cubic meters by 2050, costing China between Y5 billion and Y9 billion a year or between 1.5 and 3 percent of GDP ("China: Water Shortages" 2001). The problem is exacerbated by poor water quality. Nearly 38 percent of river waters in China were considered to be severely polluted in 2000, up from 33 percent in 1990. Among the seven major river basins, just 42 percent of the watercourses reached grade-three standards, while 28 percent failed to achieve even grade five ("Environmental Degradation" 2005). Half of such pollution comes from agriculture, especially livestock production, and the other half comes from industries and untreated water from urban areas.[35] Shortages are made more acute by inefficient use. It is estimated that China consumes four times as much water per unit of GDP as other countries ("Unquenchable Thirst" 2004). In some cities, such as Shanghai, water use per capita exceeds that of cities in Europe and Japan ("China: Water Shortages" 2001).

---

33. Consequently, China is the most water-stressed country in East Asia (World Bank 2002c).
34. Water availability in 1980 was 2,849 cubic meters per person (Shalizi 2004).
35. The share of animal husbandry in the gross value of primary production rose from 15 percent in 1970 to 26 percent in 1990 and to 34 percent in 2004. Among the industrial sectors, pulp and paper, food processing, chemicals, textiles, tanning, and mining account for close to 90 percent of the industrial chemical oxygen demand load, while contributing only 27 percent to the value of gross industrial output (Shalizi 2004).

The national average masks the large variation in the availability and use of water among different regions and sectors. Availability of water in the north is only 762 cubic meters per person compared with 3,271 cubic meters per person in the south.

Whereas in 1980, agriculture accounted for 83 percent of the water consumed, this dropped to 69 percent in 2000. Meanwhile, the share of industry rose to 21 percent. The annual growth rates for agriculture and industry were 0.1 and 4.7 percent, respectively (table 2.9). What is notable here is that, between 1980 and 2000, water use by urban residents quadrupled, although the urban population only doubled during the same period. Given the anticipated pace of urbanization, the demand for water by urban residents will only increase, and a tightening of water supplies across both sectors could slow growth.

Environmental Diseconomies

Urban industrialization and the rising use of automobiles are responsible for worsening air pollution, making China, in the words of a *Lancet* article, the "air pollution capital of the world" ("China: The Air" 2005). Yale's Center for Environmental Law and Policy ranked China near the bottom among 146 countries with regard to environmental sustainability. In 2001 two out of three cities in China failed to meet the residential ambient air quality standards of the State Environmental Protection Administration (Peng and others 2002), and a survey of 315 cities in 2004 found that one-fifth were below grade three in terms of air pollution (see tables 2.10 and 2.11). Although China has made some progress toward improving air quality, measured by the concentration of particulate matter,[36] with 37 percent of cities reaching grade two, and the concentration of sulfur dioxide, with one in five cities exceeding grade two, Chinese cities still need to redouble their efforts to improve air quality.

Estimates of the costs of pollution show large variation. The cost of air pollution (measured by damage to health and premature death) was about 7 percent of GDP in 1995 (Peng and others 2002).[37] The World Development Indicators put the costs of particulate matter and carbon

---

36. An estimated 60 percent of total suspended particulates are made up of fine particulate matter less than 10 microns in diameter, which poses greater health risks (Peng and others 2002).

37. Another estimate puts the cost at between $9 billion and $166 billion, which includes the mortality related to nitrous oxide (Brajer and Mead 2004).

Table 2.9. Water Use, by Sector, in China, 1980–2000
billion cubic meters, unless otherwise noted

Sector	1980		1993		2000		Annual growth rate, 1980–2000 (percent)
	Amount	Percent	Amount	Percent	Amount	Percent	
Total	444	100	519	100	550	100	1.1
Production	416	94	—	—	757	90	3.0
Agriculture	370	83	—	—	378	69	0.1
Industry	46	10	89	17	114	21	4.7
Domestic	28	6	—	—	57	10	3.6
Urban	6.8	1.5	24	4.6	28	5.2	7.4
Rural	21.3	4.8	—	—	29	5.3	1.6

Source: Shalizi 2004.
— Not available.

Table 2.10. Concentration of Particulates in China's Cities, by Grade, 1998, 2000, and 2002

percent, unless otherwise noted

Grade	1998	2000	2002
Grade two (reaching the standard)	32.1	36.9	36.8
Exceeding grade two	67.9	63.1	63.2
Exceeding grade three	37.7	30.3	29.8
National average (μg, microgram per cubic meter)	0.289	0.27	0.269

Source: SEPA 2003.
Note: To qualify as grade two (air quality standard for general residential areas), total suspended particulates must be less than 0.20 microgram per cubic meter, and fine particulate matter measuring less than 10 microns in diameter must be less than 0.10 microgram per cubic meter.

Table 2.11. Concentration of Sulfur Dioxide in China's Cities, by Grade, 1998, 2000, and 2002

percent, unless otherwise noted

Grade	1998	2000	2002
Grade two (reaching the standard)	70.8	78.7	77.6
Exceeding grade two	29.2	21.3	22.4
Exceeding grade three	15.2	11.7	7.9
National average (milligram per cubic meter)	0.056	0.049	0.043

Source: SEPA 2003.
Note: Grade two (air quality standard for general residential areas) is defined as sulfur dioxide less than 0.06 milligram per cubic meter. For grade three, it is less than 0.1 milligram per cubic meter.

dioxide alone at 3.1 percent of GDP in 2002. Estimates for Beijing range from 1.2 to 111 percent of city's GDP, depending on the valuation method used. Similarly, the estimates for Chongqing vary from 0.8 to 46 percent of GDP (Mao and others 2005).

In Shanghai, more than 6 million residents are exposed to sulfur dioxide and nitrogen dioxide particulate levels that are considered dangerous. The cost to the city in additional expenditures on health care is estimated to be nearly $16 billion, with 10 percent of adult deaths in the city attributable to air pollution (Kan and Chen 2004; "Pollution Costing" 2005). If the ambient air quality had been at the national level in Shijiazhuang in 2000, 251 premature deaths, 7.7 million cases of acute and chronic morbidity, and 6,589 person-years of restricted activities, amounting to 4.3 percent of GDP, could have been avoided (Peng and others 2002). In China as a whole, 100 million people live in cities where the air quality routinely becomes "very dangerous," and this pervasive problem causes more than 400,000 premature deaths annually ("China: The Air" 2005).

About 90 percent of sulfur dioxide emissions are traceable to the use of coal (Mao and others 2005). These could be cut drastically by switching to natural gas or, less effectively but more cheaply, by using low-sulfur coal (Mao and others 2005; Peng and others 2002).[38] Clean-coal technology is another alternative, but it is scale intensive and thus only available to large users of coal such as power plants. For smaller-scale users of soft coal (households and small boilers), which are the source of most low-altitude sulfur dioxide emissions, switching to natural gas would be desirable (Mao and others 2005).[39] Alongside the pollution from sulfur dioxide, there is an increasing concentration of nitrogen dioxide—a 50 percent increase in a decade—and this trend shows no signs of letting up in spite of new technologies ("Satellite View" 2005). Nitrogen dioxide has three times the warming effect of carbon dioxide, and, as it accumulates over time, the gas could accelerate the warming trend ("Something in the Air" 2006).

The high, and in some areas rising, levels of water pollution reflected in table 2.12 add to the overall grimness of the environmental picture. Possibly as many as 700 million Chinese drink water that does not meet the minimum standards of purity (Beach 2001). Whereas agriculture was once the main source of water pollution, it has been swiftly overtaken by industrial pollution caused by rural TVEs and certain types of urban industry.[40] Untreated urban sewage and wastewater and improper disposal of mushrooming urban waste in unlined landfills are compounding the problem.[41] As much as 30 billion tons of untreated sewage enter water bodies across the country each year (Beach 2001).

That these sustainability problems have come to the forefront at such a relatively early stage of development is a matter of considerable concern. After all, China's nominal GDP per capita was still just $1,730 in 2005,

---

38. For each thermal unit of output in Beijing, natural gas, Y0.17 per 1,000 kilocalories, is four times more expensive than coal, Y0.04 per 1,000 kilocalories (Mao and others 2005). Except for households, users will not see lower costs by switching to natural gas in Beijing (Mao and others 2005).

39. Although low-sulfur coal is widely available in Shijiazhuang, many still use cheaper coals. The low-emission levy on sulfur dioxide is Y200 in Shijiazhuang, while it is Y1,200 in cities such as Beijing and Guangzhou, and this may be partly to blame (Peng and others 2002).

40. Increasing production of livestock to meet the demand for meat will add to the waste produced by farmers.

41. The costs of not treating wastewater, estimated at Y4 billion in 2000, could be as high as Y23 billion in 2050 in the Hai and Hua basins (World Bank 2002a).

and over half of the population lives in rural areas. As more people move to the cities, the urban-industrial sector expands further, and the outlay on transport for passengers as well as freight increases, the growth in demand for energy, raw materials, and water will very likely continue to rise rapidly. Unless checked, pollution could worsen alongside.

When it comes to controlling the consumption per capita of both energy and water, China's options are wider than is the case for several middle-income countries. That is because China's rate of urbanization is still relatively low, and the housing, industrial, and transport infrastructure that will determine the future levels and spatial distribution of resource use as well as the quality of the environment are now being constructed. Many of today's decisions will reverberate far into the future. Undoubtedly, mistakes can be undone, but prudent choices today could mitigate waste and enable China to achieve balanced, sustainable growth at a lower cost. Policies aimed at managing the demand, including the development of technology, will have far-reaching implications for consumption, energy dependence, and, ultimately, long-run growth.

Progress toward a *xiaokang* society can be accelerated through policies implemented during the Eleventh Plan, but the economy will have to retain its growth momentum. Without this, alleviating poverty will be much harder. It also calls for an efficient management of natural resources, which could become a serious constraint, alongside a determined effort to control environmental degradation, which is adding to the costs of development.[42] A positive development that could help China come to grips with these problems is the construction of green GDP accounts. This is catching on in China, with several provinces, such as Shaanxi, attempting to account for environmental damages to and depletion of land, forestry, mineral, and water resources ("China's 'Green GDP'" 2004). One estimate of green GDP shows that the average growth of GDP between 1985 to 2000 would have been 6.5 percent, not 8.7 percent, which is obtained using the conventional measures of GDP ("China Taking" 2004).[43]

---

42. As standards of household consumption rise, resource consumption and waste disposal will pose often intractable problems (Myers and Kent 2004).

43. For a general discussion of environmental accounting and sustainability, see World Bank (2002c, ch. 2) and Lange (2003). According to the United Nations Convention to Combat Desertification, desertification costs China $6.5 billion a year ("China Taking" 2004). Thus the efforts to calculate resource and environmental costs could help China to improve efficiency in the use per unit of energy and materials ("China Taking" 2004).

Table 2.12. Water Quality in China, by Class, 1991–8

percent

Class	1991	1992	1993	1994	1995	1996	1997	1998
All China								
Classes one and two (good)	3	5	9	11	10	16	16	18
Classes three and four (moderate)	64	57	64	62	51	44	53	42
Classes five and five plus (poor)	33	38	26	27	39	40	30	40
North China								
Classes one and two (good)	4	0	6	7	6	3	7	12
Classes three and four (moderate)	56	49	61	57	41	44	53	38
Classes five and five plus (poor)	40	51	32	35	53	51	40	50
South China								
Classes one and two (good)	2	17	17	20	21	43	39	31
Classes three and four (moderate)	82	76	72	74	75	43	53	54
Classes five and five plus (poor)	16	7	11	6	4	14	7	15

Source: World Bank 2001b, p. 48.

Note: North China includes the 3-H rivers and Liao, and South China includes the Yangtze and Pearl rivers.

Global Integration and Resource Dependence

China's most widely noted impact on the global economy is through its exports of manufactured commodities. With the accession to the WTO and the phasing out of the Multi Fibre Agreement in January 2005, China's export share in manufactures such as textiles is beginning to increase at the expense of countries in Central America and South Asia.[44] But it is also becoming apparent that China's increasingly open economy is generating strong demand for imports, especially from other East Asian countries with which it runs a large trade deficit.[45] In 2003 a full 70 percent of Japan's export growth was to China, as was 40 percent of the Republic of Korea's and 90 percent of Taiwan's (China). Looking out over the balance of this decade, exports are likely to account for close to 25 percent of value added and to constitute a major component of aggregate demand. Exporting will attract FDI and, through it, the transfer of technology to China. At the same time, China will become a market that rivals the United States.

China's exports of some processed manufactures already are closely tied to the imports of components and machinery, mainly from other East and Southeast Asian countries and from the United States and Germany (Eichengreen, Rhee, and Tong 2004). China is also becoming more reliant on imported raw materials and energy from Australasia and other parts of the world.

China is the largest market for iron ore and timber exports from Australia, Brazil, and Indonesia and consumes half of the global output of cement. In 2003 China imported 150 million tons of iron ore, a 31 percent increase from 2002 ("Iron Deficiency" 2003). In 2003 the price of copper increased 25 percent and that of aluminum almost doubled, reflecting rising demand from China. The demand for steel, nickel, and

---

44. Although the impact is ameliorated by special safeguards implemented by the European Union and the United States. China and the United States reached an agreement to restrict the growth of Chinese imports to between 10 and 15 percent in 2006, between 12.5 and 16 percent in 2007, and between 15 and 17 percent in 2008 ("China, US Sign" 2005). Many countries in Southeast and South Asia saw double-digit growth of garment and textile exports because many apparel firms anticipated the protectionist stances taken by the European Union and the United States and established sources in other countries. In addition, Chinese firms had invested $715 million in 114 factories abroad by 2004 ("International: China Textile Talks" 2005).
45. The compound aggregate growth rate (CAGR) of exports from ASEAN (Association of South East Asian Nations) to China was 28 percent a year between 1999 and 2003. China's exports averaged a CAGR of 26 percent.

copper increased dramatically between 2000 and 2003, and much of the rise was because of China's increasing demand: 95 percent for steel, 99 percent for nickel, and 100 percent for copper ("Iron Deficiency" 2003). While imports of food and feed grain are fairly modest, as China's consumption of meat increases—China accounts for 28 percent of total meat consumption worldwide but still only 50 kilograms per capita compared with 122 kilograms in the United States—imports of feed grains and of wheat will rise (Myers and Kent 2004; World Bank 2004b). Furthermore, increasing traffic of raw materials to China has resulted in the shortage of bulk carriers from Australia, Brazil, and other parts of East Asia ("Iron Deficiency" 2003).[46] Similarly, growing demand for energy is increasing China's dependence on petroleum imports from the Middle East—close to 50 percent of the total imported in 2003—and has contributed both to the rising prices of oil and to the high rates for chartering oil tankers ("China: A Five-Year Outlook" 2004; "Oil and Politics" 2004).

At GDP growth averaging 8 percent or more, China's importance as a trading nation will rise sharply during the balance of the decade. Exports will remain a driver of industrial demand, and the pattern of China's trade will matter increasingly, most directly for East Asian countries but for other economies as well. China's demand for raw materials will also begin to affect prices and global production to a far greater degree. These developments will call for policy actions regarding trading relationships and also regarding energy and commodity dependence.

---

46. China is the largest consumer of copper in the world, and its demand moves international copper prices. In the first half of 2004, the premium at Shanghai was $150 per million tons over the price on the London Metal Exchange, diverting materials from the European Union and the United States to the Chinese market ("International: Prices to Rise" 2004). A trading scandal involving a Chinese trader in November 2005 highlighted China's role in the global copper market. In order to secure a steady supply, the Chinese government is encouraging firms to seek mines abroad, although a bid to secure a copper mine in South Africa failed ("As Demand Grows" 2004). Similarly, Chinese demand affects the price movement of aluminum, especially the expectation that power shortages will curtail domestic production ("International: Metal Supply" 2004). China is also the largest consumer and producer of cotton in the world, satisfying part of its requirements from imports ("Cotton in China" 2004). Growth of China's auto industry has led to a spike in the demand for tires and a shortage of natural rubber and steel cord ("Tyre Industry" 2004).

PART 2

Policies for Rapid, Balanced, and Sustainable Growth

CHAPTER 3

Sustaining Growth

Growth needs to be viewed from two angles: (a) the contribution of resource inputs and factor productivity to the longer-run expansion of GDP and (b) the pull exerted by increasing aggregate demand on growth. Both supply and demand forces must operate in tandem for a country to reach its growth objectives, and while this report emphasizes the supply side, management of demand will require equal attention from the authorities. Before examining some of the key factors that are likely to underpin China's future growth, it is important to underline the uniqueness of China's recent experience.

No other country has averaged a growth rate of more than 9 percent over a 25-year period. Others that approximately match China's record are Japan, Korea, and Thailand, all drawn from a small group of economies that are charter members of the East Asian Miracle Club. When Easterly and others (1993) reviewed the growth experience of a large sample of countries, they found that consistently high growth rates are an anomaly and limited to a handful of economies in East Asia. Elsewhere, there is a strong tendency for economies to regress toward a mean global rate. Growth spurts tend to peter out after a few years. For a spurt to extend over decades is extraordinary, especially for a country as large as China. Hence it is necessary to strike a note of caution. While we argue in this report that China has the potential to sustain high rates of growth, there is no precedent to guide us. A weakening of domestic demand or a sharp slowdown of foreign demand as a result of an international crisis could break China's momentum. So could a severe financial crisis or prolonged or widespread and debilitating civil unrest sparked by perceptions of economic injustice and corruption. All these and others have been frequently aired and serve as a warning against taking China's rapid growth for granted. As in the past, growth will depend on good policies, the crafting of reforms to remedy institutional weaknesses, and good luck.

Supply-Side Developments

Past analyses of China's growth have rightly concentrated on factor inputs and total factor productivity (TFP) spurred by structural changes and market reforms. Of these, capital investment that introduces embodied technical change, the infusion of skills, and total factor productivity will be the dominant sources of growth over the foreseeable future. TFP, which currently accounts for less than a third of growth (based on growth accounting), should increase its share, and we return to this below. FDI will continue to play a role, and its contribution could rise in significance as China comes to rely increasingly on technology to sustain growth.

A decomposition of the sources of growth in China, by Heytens and Zebregs (2003), is instructive and underscores the importance of reforms that could enlarge the share of TFP in the future. Table 3.1 shows that, between 1979 and 1998, capital accumulation contributed the bulk of growth. This accounting framework is likely to exaggerate the role of capital and to downplay the role of embodied technical change. The contribution of capital (and of embodied technical progress) to output growth rose from 63 percent in 1979–89 to 67 percent in 1990–8. The contribution of TFP (in accounting terms) rose from 2.78 percent in 1979–84, when agricultural reforms were initiated, to 2.81 percent in 1990–4, when the third round of reforms focused on decontrol and "marketization" accelerated, before declining to 2.30 percent during 1995–8. Comparable results for 1993–4 were obtained by Kuijs and Wang (2005). They found that TFP accounted for 30 percent of the growth (2–7 percentage points) and capital accumulation for 62 percent. During 1993–2004, Kuijs and Wang peg the growth of IFP at 2.7 percent, which is close to the 2.5 percent estimate of Jorgenson and Vu (2005) for 1995–2004.

A decomposition of the productivity numbers shows that between 70 percent (1979–84) and 90 percent (1995–98) of the gains were derived

Table 3.1. Contributions to Output Growth in China, 1971–2004
percent of GDP (period average)

Contributor	1971–8	1979–89	1990–8	1993–2004ᵃ
Actual output growth	5.4	9.1	9.5	9.0
Capital accumulation	4.8	5.7	6.4	5.1
Labor force growth	0.7	1.0	0.5	1.1
TFP growth	−0.5	2.5	2.6	2.7

Source: Heytens and Zebregs 2003; Kuijs and Wang 2005.
a. From Kuijs and Wang 2005.

from the transfer of labor out of the primary sector and into urban sector jobs that harnessed modern technologies to yield significantly greater value added (see table 3.2). Structural reforms contributed one-third of TFP growth in the earlier period and 17 percent in 1995–8 (Heytens and Zebregs 2003).[1] What this decomposition suggests is that the scope for productivity gains from embodied and disembodied technical change is large as a result of increased spending on research and development (R&D), continuing modernization of the capital stock, and innovation in organization, management, and process technologies, a point we explore later in this chapter.

Demand-Led Growth

To realize the growth potential inherent in higher factor inputs and TFP, China must generate demand that will impel increased production. During the past decade, the growth of investment and consumption has been the principal driver, with net exports providing an additional boost in some years (see table 3.3).

Looking ahead, investment, particularly in infrastructure, urban housing, and industry will remain important, but there is little room for the ratio of investment to GDP—already in excess of 42 percent—to rise further.[2] It is likely that the composition of investment will shift even more toward housing and urban infrastructure to accommodate the massive

---

1. Heytens and Zebregs (2003) measure the results of reforms; see their appendix 3 for details on how they constructed these variables.
2. It is believed that Chinese firms are overinvesting in certain manufacturing activities—for example, steel and white goods—and that this has created an overhang of excess industrial capacity, especially in consumer durables. Financial market distortion might be largely to blame, coupled with the size of the public sector, which is the main user of financial resources ("Chronic Overinvestment" 2003; "Too Fast" 2006).

Table 3.2. Contributions to TFP Growth in China, 1971–1998

percent of TFP (period average)

Contributor	1971–8	1979–84	1985–9	1990–4	1995–8
TFP growth	−0.53	2.78	2.11	2.81	2.30
Structural reform	0.38	0.94	0.76	0.83	0.39
Labor migration out of primary sector	2.34	2.01	1.52	2.15	2.08
Exogenous trend	−3.25	−0.17	−0.17	−0.17	−0.17

Source: Heytens and Zebregs 2003.

Table 3.3. Growth Rate of GDP in China, by Source, 1990–2003

percent

Year	GDP	Consumption	Government spending	Investment	Imports	Exports
1990	3.8	1.1	1.1	−0.1	0.0	4.3
1991	9.2	4.7	2.6	2.8	2.8	2.4
1992	14.2	6.9	1.8	4.4	5.3	2.0
1993	13.5	4.4	1.2	9.3	8.7	2.4
1994	12.6	3.4	1.1	6.0	2.3	5.0
1995	10.5	4.5	0.7	6.2	1.6	1.2
1996	9.6	5.5	0.3	3.1	0.2	−0.1
1997	8.8	2.4	0.9	1.9	2.2	4.4
1998	7.8	3.0	1.1	2.4	0.6	1.4
1999	7.1	3.5	1.3	2.3	4.9	3.1
2001	8.0	3.8	1.5	1.8	6.1	7.7
2002	7.5	2.7	1.3	5.4	2.8	2.5
2003	8.0	2.8	0.9	5.4	8.3	9.0

Source: Data derived from World Bank 2003a.

anticipated influx of people into China's cities. Similarly, while China's exports will continue expanding, given the scale already reached, the rate of increase is bound to diminish. In 2004 China's exports grew more than 35 percent to reach $596 billion, pushing China into third place among exporting nations ("China's Trade Surplus" 2005). They increased by 28.4 percent in 2005 and stood at $762 billion by the end of the year ("China: Soaring Exports" 2006). Over the longer term, rates of growth comparable to those attained in the recent past are unlikely, but assuming that the global economy remains buoyant, exports could continue to increase between 15 and 20 percent for a few more years. These rates of growth would raise the ratio of exports to GDP from 37 percent in 2004[3] to

---

3. Based on estimated GDP of $1.6 trillion in 2004 (Economist Intelligence Unit 2004). This was adjusted to $2.23 trillion in 2005.

between 40 and 50 percent by the end of the decade, or close to that of smaller industrializing countries, such as Korea and Thailand. Meanwhile, imports are booming, but still growing less than exports.[4] At the same time, with increasing income, the relative price of nontradables is bound to rise, thereby reducing the share of trade in GDP. Thus the net effect of the trading sector on domestic demand could begin falling over the course of the decade.

In this scenario—and under most conceivable future circumstances—consumption will be the principal driver of growth, with investment a close second. Consumption has been reasonably buoyant, but its share of GDP in China stood at 61 percent in 2004 (table 3.4), much lower than the global average of 78 percent. Three factors have raised the propensity of households to save since the early 1980s. First is the rapid growth of incomes, which, for reasons indicated by the life-cycle hypothesis, translates into high rates of saving. Second is the decline in family size, resulting from the one-child policy, which has induced individuals to save for retirement, adjusted for longer life expectancy. The third and related factor is the absence of a national social security system that would provide adequate pension benefits for urban and rural households alike

Table 3.4. Final Consumption as a Share of GDP, 1980–2004

Year	Percent of GDP
1980	65.4
1985	65.7
1990	62.0
1995	57.5
2000	61.1
2001	59.8
2002	58.2
2003	61.2
2004	60.5

Source: National Bureau of Statistics of China, *China Statistical Yearbook,* 2004.

4. The 2.1 percent appreciation of the yuan in 2005 did little to slow the expansion of exports. However, a significant realignment of China's exchange rate relative to the dollar and other East Asian currencies and a shift in demand toward domestic consumption could narrow the trade gap. Two points should be noted. First, the appreciation of the Japanese yen did not do away with Japan's trade surplus, trade imbalances with the United States, or reliance on exports for growth. Second, China's trade gap with other East Asian countries will depend on the degree to which these currencies adjust relative to the renminbi.

(Modigliani and Cao 2004). A strengthening of the social safety net is likely to raise the propensity to consume over time.

Is there a case for incentives to stimulate household consumption during the Eleventh Plan period? In answering this question, we need to weigh four considerations.[5] First, in order to provide jobs for new entrants and the unemployed in urban as well as rural areas, China will need to sustain growth rates in the 8–9 percent range. This pace is also affected by declining employment elasticity in the manufacturing sector (for staff and workers and broadly for all employed persons as well) and in the high-value-adding producer services, where the potential for productivity gains is large (see tables 3.5 and 3.6). Countering this is a second consideration that arises from the perception of economic overheating in 2003–5, during which GDP growth averaged 10 percent, which raised inflation to more than 5 percent in 2004, and from numerous infrastructure bottlenecks.[6] In fact, half of all Chinese provinces experienced power shortages during 2003–4. The overheating is ascribed mainly to a sharp rise in investment (spending on fixed assets rose 28 percent in the first three quarters of 2004) and higher spending by households on cars and durables, assisted by easier access to consumer financing from banks ("China: A Five-Year Outlook" 2004). Consumer credit doubled over the past two years, even though it still accounts for less than 1 percent of bank loans. In the second half of 2004, concern over the state of the economy and losses from consumer financing prompted the authorities to raise interest rates and tighten credit, including to consumers. Thus, in the medium term, demand is likely to be strong, and further inducements might not be needed to attain the desired growth rates of GDP.

This brings us to the third consideration, which relates to the use of financial incentives (consumer financing, credit cards) to stimulate consumer demand and lower household saving propensities. Although saving rates in China are high, their stability at or near current levels should not

---

5. Of particular importance is the emergence of a middle stratum of households in China. They each have incomes of $9,000 or more and assets of $37,000 or more and account for 19 percent of the population. Their demand for housing and durable goods will be a big factor in aggregate consumer demand, especially because the stratum will comprise 40 percent of the population by 2020, and their average incomes will be in the $18,000 range ("Dissecting China's Middle Stratum" 2004).

6. By one estimate, road congestion was causing annual losses of $4 billion to $6 billion, and this was compounded by congestion in the main ports ("South-East Asia: China Boom" 2004). However, these are likely to be ameliorated through investment in infrastructur and energy, which amounts to 20 percent of GDP (Lee 2005).

Table 3.5. Labor Elasticity in Manufacturing in China, 1989–2004

Year	Employed persons			Staff and workers			Growth rate of manufacturing output[a]
	Number (10,000)	Growth rate (percent)	Labor elasticity	Number (10,000)	Growth rate (percent)	Labor elasticity	
1989	8,547	—	—	5,206	—	—	—
1990	8,624	0.90	0.39	5,304	1.88	0.82	2.30
1991	8,839	2.49	0.20	5,443	2.62	0.21	12.60
1992	9,106	3.02	0.16	5,508	1.19	0.06	18.70
1993	9,295	2.08	0.11	5,469	-0.71	-0.04	18.60
1994	9,613	3.42	0.2	5,434	-0.64	-0.04	17.00
1995	9,803	1.98	0.16	5,439	0.09	0.01	12.40
1996	9,763	-0.41	-0.04	5,293	-2.68	-0.24	11.10
1997	9,612	-1.55	-0.16	5,083	-3.97	-0.42	9.40
1998	8,319	-13.45	-1.66	3,769	-25.85	-3.19	8.10
1999	8,109	-2.52	-0.30	3,496	-7.24	-0.85	8.50
2000	8,043	-0.81	-0.08	3,240	-7.32	-0.69	10.60
2001	8,083	0.50	0.06	3,010	-7.10	-0.84	8.50
2002	8,307	2.77	0.27	2,907	-3.42	-0.34	10.10
2003	—	—	—	2,899	-0.28	—	—
2004	—	—	—	2,960	2.10	—	—

Source: National Bureau of Statistics of China, *China's Statistical Yearbook*, various years; National Bureau of Statistics of China and others 2004.
— Not available.
a. Data derived from World Bank 2003a.

Table 3.6. Labor Elasticity of Output in China, by Sector, 1981–2003

Year	Primary	Secondary	Industry	Tertiary
1981–5	0.094	0.477	0.218	0.400
1986–90	1.083	0.438	0.186	0.636
1991–5	−0.404	0.095	0.007	0.598
1996–2000	0.190	0.002	−0.583	0.218
1998–2003	0.204	−0.041	−0.361	0.270

Source: Primary, secondary, and tertiary employment data are derived from the employment section of various issues of *A Statistical Abstract of China,* National Bureau of Statistics of China. Industry employment data are derived
from tables on the number of staff and workers in industry in National Bureau of Statistics of China, *China Statistical
Yearbook,* various years, except for 1981 data, which are calculated from the employment section.

Figure 3.1. Household Saving Rates in China, Japan, and Korea, 1953–2003

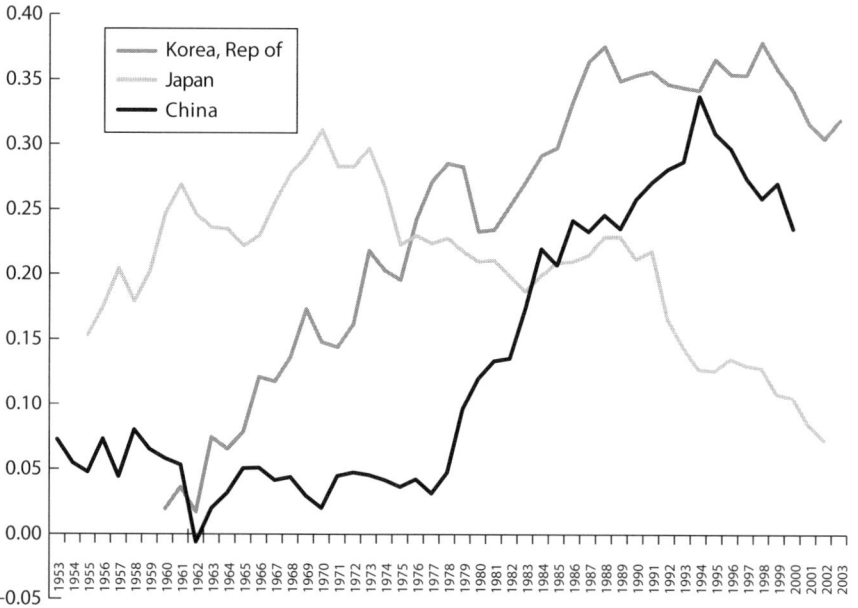

Source: World Bank 2005c.

be taken as a given. In both Japan and Korea, changes in the incentives
regime for households and in demographic circumstances have led to
steep declines in a matter of years, as can be seen in figure 3.1. Japanese
households have appreciably reduced their savings, and even the savings
of Korean households are far below the peak reached in 1998. Moreover,
Korean consumers are awash in debt as a result of imprudent consumer
loan and credit card schemes introduced in the latter part of the 1990s to

stimulate demand. In view of China's level of development, the inadequacy of the social security system, the rising costs of medical care, and the massive unsatisfied need for infrastructure, any significant increase in consumption propensities could contribute to excess demand and eat away at the supply of investible resources.[7]

The fourth consideration following directly from the above is that, aside from financing continuing industrialization, China must finance urban development on a vast scale over the coming decade. Upgrading the existing stock of housing and infrastructure and providing housing and services for between 150 million and 200 million people who will be moving to cities will absorb a large volume of investment. Automobile transportation, water, and energy for urban residents will also require substantial amounts of capital. In other words, investment opportunities should be plentiful, and it is difficult to foresee a chronic shortage of demand during the next 10 years, which would call for policies to enlarge consumer spending further.

China would benefit from regulatory and financial reforms (for example, a deepening of the market for home mortgages) and market integration to enhance the efficiency of resource use. In addition, demand management will be needed to smooth the bumps from temporary overheating and softening of demand, but it would appear that the demand-side picture does not warrant policy actions to increase consumption propensities in a sustained manner.

Meanwhile, consumption growth could be fed by other developments as well. The share of household income in the economy is bound to rise, a pattern observed in other countries, making way for higher consumption. Furthermore, government consumption, which is still modest, is likely to increase if policy attention begins to shift from economic construction to higher spending on health, education, and income transfer schemes. Together, these likely trends make a more active policy of stimulating consumption less desirable.

Sectoral Sources of Growth

A sectoral perspective indicates that industry—in particular, manufacturing—will be the most important source of growth because of its

---

7. A survey of 6,000 Chinese households brought to light a lack of confidence regarding future financial security and a marked tendency to save for retirement and unforeseen contingency. More than half of the households surveyed saved all or most of the increase in their earnings over the past year (Lane and St-Maurice 2006).

weight in the economy and its momentum (see table 3.7), both of which can be sustained for at least a decade:[8] China accounted for a little more than 5 percent of global manufacturing in 2001, compared with 20 percent for the United States ("Made in China" 2005). However, as table 3.5 shows, the employment elasticity for manufacturing is quite low, and total employment in the sector is declining (see table 3.8). This is

Table 3.7. GDP Growth in China, by Sector, 1980–2004

Year	GDP growth rate	Primary	Secondary	Industry	Tertiary
1980	7.8	−0.5	6.6	5.6	1.3
1985	13.5	0.5	8.0	7.0	5.2
1990	3.8	1.6	1.6	1.5	0.7
1995	13.1	0.8	8.6	7.6	3.7
2000	7.6	0.5	3.7	3.4	3.5
2001	8.4	0.4	4.3	3.9	3.8
2002	8.3	0.4	3.8	3.5	4.2
2003	9.1	0.4	4.4	3.9	4.3
2004	10.0	0.3	5.8	5.2	3.9

Source: National Bureau of Statistics of China, *China Statistical Yearbook*, 1981, 1986, 2005.
Note: Updated figures are used after 1995.

Table 3.8: Share of Employment in Three Sectors

Year	Primary Industry	Secondary Industry	Manu facturing	Tertiary Industry
1989	60.1%	21.6%	15.3%	18.3%
1990	60.1%	21.4%	13.2%	18.5%
1991	59.7%	21.4%	13.4%	18.9%
1992	58.5%	21.7%	13.6%	19.8%
1993	56.4%	22.4%	13.8%	21.2%
1994	54.3%	22.7%	14.1%	23.0%
1995	52.2%	23.0%	14.2%	24.8%
1996	50.5%	23.5%	14.0%	26.0%
1997	49.9%	23.7%	13.6%	26.4%
1998	49.8%	23.5%	11.5%	26.7%
1999	50.1%	23.0%	11.1%	26.9%
2000	50.0%	22.5%	10.9%	27.5%
2001	50.0%	22.3%	10.9%	27.7%
2002	50.0%	21.4%	11.0%	28.6%
2003	49.1%	21.6%		29.3%
2004	46.9%	22.5%		30.6%

Source: *China Statistical Yearbook* (2005)

---

8. A recent report by the OECD (2005b) maintains that the biggest source of growth within the commercial business sector are private businesses, the share of which in output has risen to 63 percent from 54 percent in 1998.

because of the capital and skill bias of technological change and increasing productivity.

The tertiary sector is next in importance. In recent years, it has contributed about a third of growth. This share will rise as its weight in the economy, which was 41 percent in 2004,[9] expands. Moreover, it will be responsible for an increasing share of employment, as is the case in other industrializing and developed economies. But because of advances in information technology and numerous process innovations, productivity in services such as retailing, wholesaling, finance, and logistics is rising. Hence, it is reasonable to expect that employment elasticity in tertiary industries will continue trending down, as can be seen in table 3.6.

The primary sector is now responsible for just 13 percent of GDP, and this will shrink to between 10 and 12 percent by 2010. However, agriculture employs almost 42 percent of the workforce, and most of the poor live in rural areas. For this reason, growth of agricultural incomes takes on a disproportionate significance. China's cultivated acreage is constrained by the scarcity of arable land, water shortages, and urbanization, which is encroaching on land in the vicinity of cities (see table 3.9). Future growth will come mainly from higher crop yields and changes in the mix of crops produced.

Yields of various crops in China are high relative to China's main comparators (see table 3.10). For example, rice yields are close to those of Japan and the United States and well above those of Vietnam. Yields of wheat match those in the United States. This is achieved through the use of improved seeds and the heavy application of fertilizers.[10] By using agricultural extension services effectively, farmers in China have introduced new varietals and exploited biogenetic technologies, bringing them close to the technological frontier for food grains (Jin and others 2002).[11]

---

9. This does not include construction, which accounted for 5.4 percent of GDP in 2004, according to the adjusted GDP data released at the end of 2005. The value added contributed by the service sector was revised upward by 49 percent in the new data. In 1993 it had been revised upward by 32 percent (Holz 2006).

10. Farmers in China use 228 kilograms of plant nutrients per hectare, as opposed to the world average of 90 kilograms in 2002 (FAO 2003).

11. This is especially true for rice. The gap between the potential and actual yield is only 15 percent of the yield. When compared with countries such as India, with 58 percent, or the Philippines, with 65 percent, China's gap of 15 percent for rice is extremely small (Jin and others 2002). According to Liu and Wang (2005), between 1991 and 1999, technological advances were responsible for more than half of agricultural productivity growth.

Table 3.9. Total Cultivated Land in China, 1980–2004
thousands of hectares

Year	Land cultivated
1980	99,305
1985	96,846
1990	95,672
1995	94,970
1996[a]	130,039
2001	127,082
2004	130,040

Source: National Bureau of Statistics of China, *China Statistical Yearbook,* various years.
Note: Figures from 1980 to 1995 are estimates.
a. Data for 1996 are from the Ministry of Land and Resource and from the 1996 agricultural census reported in *China Statistical Yearbook.*

Table 3.10. Yield per Hectare for Select Grains in Select Countries, Various Years

Crop and period covered	Country	Yield per hectare (tons)
Rice, 2002	China	6.3
	Japan	6.6
	Thailand	2.6
	Vietnam	4.6
	United States	7.4
	Asia	4.0
	World	3.9
Wheat, 1998–2000	China	3.8
	Argentina	2.5
	Canada	2.4
	Russia	1.6
	United States	2.9
	East Asia	3.8
	World	2.7
Maize, 1997–9	China	4.9
	Argentina	2.4
	Brazil	5.3
	Mexico	2.7
	United States	8.3
	East Asia	4.8
	World	4.3

Source: Ekboir 2002; Pingali 2001.
Note: Data for rice from World Rice Statistics, prepared by International Rice Research Institute.

Although a slow increase in yields cannot be ruled out, future gains in farm incomes are likely to come from a greater emphasis on horticulture and animal husbandry. Such shifts, along with any consolidation of farms into larger holdings in order to realize scale economies, will lead to more capital-intensive farming practices that will whittle down employment in agriculture. The shift in the crop mix will promote exports, 70 percent of which comprise horticulture, animal, and aquaculture products (Rosen, Rozelle, and Huang 2004).

Farmers in the eastern and central regions will gain more than those in the western region. They will boost their output by 20–100 percent more than farmers in the western region. In addition, richer farmers will tend to gain more, again because they tend to produce commodities whose terms of trade are expected to rise under the WTO (Rosen, Rozelle, and Huang 2004). In fact, 74 percent of richer farmers grow agricultural products that are competitive under the WTO, while only 36 percent of poor farmers in the west do so (Huang, Li, and Rozelle 2003).

While China must emphasize the structural, institutional, and policy issues that influence the input side of the growth equation, managing demand through short- and medium-term macro policies will remain vital for these other policies to deliver results.

Rapid growth calls for a few major reform initiatives of a strategic nature. International evidence suggests that, once a country has substantially deregulated the economy, bold reforms are more likely to impart long-term momentum than incremental policy changes (Hausmann, Pritchett, and Rodrik 2004; OECD 2004b). In this spirit, China could significantly extend current reforms in three areas:

- urbanization
- the innovation system, IT, FDI, and trade
- state enterprises and the banking sector.

Pattern of Urban Development and Agglomeration Effects

In the medium run, increased factor productivity will derive principally from the transfer of labor from the rural to the urban areas.[12] The intersectoral shift will raise labor productivity and also the returns to capital in urban areas. Substantial gains in productivity can arise, in addition,

---

12. Fogel (2004) estimates that 30 percent of the increase in productivity will come from this source.

from urban agglomeration economies. Thus urbanization and policies that enhance the gains from urban development should be considered the central elements of China's growth strategy.

The growth potential inherent in urbanization can be augmented by concentrating the population in large metropolitan centers and maximizing the resulting agglomeration economies, which can range from 3 to 14 percent in city GDP for each doubling of city size (Rosenthal and Strange 2003). The size of urban centers can be a big plus.[13] Agglomeration effects include economies of scale and scope, linkage effects, the gains from industrial diversity, "thick" labor markets, innovation made possible by the clustering of firms, science and technology workers, and research institutions, and the emergence of local business and social cultures that enable individuals to work together more effectively (Scott 2001; Scott and Storper 2003). By comparison, dispersed urbanization in a continental-size country can be costly in terms of land use (especially when arable land is scarce, as in China), investment in infrastructure, and energy intensity. The tendency observed worldwide is for urban growth to be concentrated in the coastal areas, along major waterways, and at key transport junctions. In the United States, more than half of the population now lives within 50 miles of a coastline and, over time, has moved from colder to relatively warmer parts of the country.[14] In China, also, migration flows have been oriented toward the large cities, especially those along the coast and, to a lesser extent, at major waterways and transport nodes. If national policy were to reinforce this tendency, the outcome over time would likely be the emergence of a few densely populated urban regions, the distribution increasingly determined by locational advantages, climate, and the availability of adequate water supplies.

The positive aspect of such development is that large urban centers can be the focus of growth for the national economy and key nodes in the global economic system. Furthermore, in polycentric metropolitan regions, the advantages of size need not be undermined by excessive congestion along a few corridors radiating from a central core—such metropolitan areas have several business districts.[15] In China's case, increasing

---

13. See recent reviews of the literature on agglomeration by Baldwin and Martin (2003); and Rosenthal and Strange (2003).
14. See Glaeser and Shapiro (2001); Rappaport and Sachs (2003).
15. Although as traffic levels rise, sustaining the advantages of size will require careful regulation, efficient pricing of congestion, investment in infrastructure, and a balance between public and private transport (and rail and road solutions) to arrive at desirable outcomes. On this, see Downs (2004).

the size of cities promises productivity dividends, and, if the diseconomies of scale can be avoided by good planning and sound regulation, cities can grow very large and still remain efficient.[16]

A greater concentration of the population in metropolitan regions, mainly in the eastern coastal provinces, is not without risks. Cities often have difficulty coping with a large influx of migrants,[17] which strains social services and the safety net (a point we develop later in this chapter) as well as the physical infrastructure. Migration can lead to the formation of ghettos and cause environmental problems that undercut the benefits of agglomeration economies. A policy emphasizing large urban centers could also disadvantage some of the medium and smaller cities in the hinterland by draining resources and potentially widening inter-city income differentials. The outcome would be influenced by the number and type of jobs created as well as the intergovernmental fiscal system, which can offset some of these income differentials or at least their effects on the capacity of the hinterland to deliver services.

If managed well, these risks are more than offset by the benefits of agglomeration. Available evidence suggests that the efficient strategy would be to develop the existing dynamic urban regions, since many of them are suboptimal in size (Henderson 2004a). While this might affect the fortunes of some urban areas with few locational advantages, by and large, given the anticipated flow of people to large cities, the pain is likely to be localized, and sending areas stand to benefit from reduced pressures on the land and higher remittances. The potential efficiency gains from integrating the national labor market and realizing agglomeration economies from bigger cities can be fairly large. They range from 4.1 percent if the current city size is only 20 percent of the optimal to a gain of 35 percent if the current size is half of the optimal size (see table 3.11).[18]

A national economy in which industrial activity is increasingly concentrated in large metropolitan areas mainly in the east, southeast, and along the Yangtze region will be easier to integrate into a unified national market. Such urban regions will have the advantage of geographic contiguity and will provide a more competitive environment, dense and flexible labor markets, modern physical infrastructure, diverse sources of financing that permit ease of entry for new firms, and a much broader fiscal base

---

16. For the benefits, see Henderson (2004b).
17. See, for instance, Davis (2004) on the proliferation of slum areas.
18. Other estimates range from 13 to 30 percent of GDP (see Whalley and Zhang 2004 and Chen 2001, respectively).

Table 3.11. Potential Gains from Optimizing City Size in China
percent

Current size as a percent of the optimum	Gain in value added per worker
50	35.0
40	20.0
30	9.5
20	4.1

Source: Henderson 2004a.

for the local authorities. All of these diminish the incentives for subnational governments to protect local enterprises through trade barriers and preferential contracts or to support them with directed credit. Such behavior is much more likely in the smaller urban centers dependent on a limited number of businesses.

Tokyo is in many ways an example of a successful metropolitan region, attracting migrants from other parts of Japan since the early 1950s. It accounts for well over a fifth of Japan's population and has remained the dynamic hub of the economy, possibly because it has efficiently absorbed such a large influx of population and benefited from a virtuous cycle of agglomeration economies. The experience of the Tokyo metropolitan region could inform the development of China's major coastal cities. During 1950–70, Tokyo's growth was pegged to Japan's electrical, mechanical, and transport industries as well as others, which brought into existence an enormously diversified base of industry embracing 122 of a possible 125 three-digit subsectors. The transport system that evolved during this period reinforced Tokyo's dominance by providing easy access to other parts of the country (Fujita and others 2004).

These developments induced a sizable fraction of the larger companies to locate their headquarters in Tokyo and galvanized the business services sector. As Japan has moved into a postindustrial era, Tokyo has widened its lead over the next largest city, Osaka, because agglomeration economies have proven to be even more potent for high-tech manufacturing, advanced producer services, and the creative industries that are the lifeblood of Tokyo's economy in the early twenty-first century. Companies that rely more on research and on innovation to remain competitive are finding that it helps to keep their head offices, their principal research facilities, and their key manufacturing plants in and around Tokyo. This is because the success of innovative activities now depends on proximity to suppliers of many complementary design, production, legal, financial, marketing, and engineering services and close proximity to a huge metropolitan market where new products can be launched and tested (Bresnahan, Gambardella, and Saxenian 2001; Fujita and Hill 2005). Innovation is associated, in addition, with the presence of research-oriented universities that are a source of skills and of basic research that supports narrower, more applied research into commercializable innovations conducted mainly by firms. Agglomeration makes possible frequent face-to-face interaction, which remains the preferred channel through which most tacit knowledge is exchanged and business transactions are conducted. Because they are not codified, the latest research findings diffuse slowly, mostly through face-to-face exchanges (Leamer and Storper 2001; Storper and Venables 2002). Large metropolitan areas can provide a multiplicity of attractive venues for close interaction, but much depends on the quality of the urban environment and whether it offers the mix of amenities conducive to such interaction (Adams 2002; Florida 2002; Keller 2002).

Research on Tokyo and other large metropolitan areas underscores the contribution of an effective intra- and inter-city public transport system to the fruition of agglomeration economies and the efficiency of land use. The transport system has an important role because it is the principal component of a modern logistics system and hence contributes to the industrial competitiveness of an urban center.[19]

Intra-metropolitan transport and other public services such as sanitation and waste management also influence the quality of the urban environment through their impact on traffic congestion and pollution. In both these respects, Tokyo and, on a smaller scale, Singapore are pacesetters in the East Asian context.

Transport and other public utilities are capital intensive, and developing them requires long-term financing. In China much of this still comes from the banking sector, with an explicit or implicit local government guarantee. However, other types of term financing would be much more appropriate (Honohan 2004). Where the financial resources are raised by contractors, local governments often do not have much control over design nor can they easily monitor the spending of borrowed funds. Furthermore, once contractors foresee that a project might fail, they have an incentive to divert resources to themselves, leaving the local banks and governments to shoulder the cost of the unfinished project (Bird 2004; Honohan 2004). Thus current lending arrangements are inefficient and

---

19. The congestion can be mitigated by adopting electronic road pricing and synchronized signals.

risky. Instead, governments could shift some of the risks associated with infrastructure investments to investors through structured bond financing, which is often attractive, and to institutional investors such as insurance companies (Honohan 2004).[20]

The tax system that is needed to finance urban growth and services plays an equally important role. Perhaps most important, the way real estate is taxed can influence the efficiency of land use. If a property tax is adopted, it will lead to low-density urban development, whereas if a "land-only" tax is adopted, it will lead to denser development. The use of "highest and best use" as the tax base will most probably result in denser development and likely yield the most efficient use of the land (Bird 2004). Thus by varying the degree to which land and improvements on land (property) are taxed, the municipal authorities can influence how the city will evolve (sprawling or with a denser urban center).[21]

More broadly, allowing cities more flexibility in setting rates of taxation would provide those that are growing with the means to appropriate some of the agglomeration effects in order to finance growth and services. This would reduce some of the pressures on periurban land, which is being converted at an unsustainable rate, with negative implications for food security and farmers' property rights, mainly because land conversion constitutes a large source of revenue for local governments.

If, indeed, much of the growth of the economy is to come from urbanization and agglomeration, government should refurbish the intergovernmental fiscal system to allow for some redistribution of revenues. Failing to do so would undermine the hinterland's capacity to deliver public services in sufficient quantities to those left behind. In the end, it could

---

20. In order to finance infrastructure projects through bond issuance, a number of other market features must be present, such as the transparency of municipal governance, the bond rating of municipal governments, and the liberalization of interest rates. In October 2004, the government began liberalizing interest rates ("China: Interest Reforms" 2004). In general, interest rates are negatively correlated with the size of the city, enabling large cities to have better access to bond markets at lower cost (Bird 2004). Currently, local governments are prohibited from borrowing directly from banks. However, without adequate fiscal resources, many local governments are relying on quasi-government entities to raise financing for infrastructure and other services, and these do manage to obtain funding from banks (Dabla-Norris 2004; World Bank 2003c).

21. Zhu (2004) discusses issues connected to the leasing of urban land and the use of land development rights in Shanghai.

even undermine migration to the cities themselves, because of the lack of services, such as education, that better prepare migrants for the move to the city.[22]

Finally, to allow the benefits from urbanization and agglomeration to spread throughout the economy, China must reinforce its efforts to further integrate the national economy, a process that has been ongoing but gradual.[23] Trade is hindered by the inadequacy of logistics (none of the 18,000 logistics providers in China offers nationwide service), by the inconvenience and cost of shipment (on nonbulk commodities) by rail, by taxes on road transport, and by continuing tax and other impediments on the use of containers within and across transport modes. One part of the solution lies in building the physical infrastructure that will knit provincial markets together more tightly into a national market.[24] This is being done and should continue to receive priority. The road network, for example, at 1.76 million kilometers, is barely sufficient, the 35,000-kilometer trunk highway system is at an early stage of development, and the waterway network has, because of neglect, shrunk to only a fraction of what it was in 1960. The railway system, with 74,000 kilometers of track, is also under great pressure and needs to be expanded and made more efficient through much greater use of information technology (such as bar codes and tracking), less transportation of coal (which would result from better energy policies and a national power grid), and reform of selective ownership to permit other providers to offer some services.[25]

The second part of the solution is the most complex and a desirable focus of the Eleventh Plan strategy. China still lacks an effective regulatory system to identify, penalize, and strike down illegal local rules, contracting arrangements, subsidies, and levies on imported items in what is fun-

---

22. Already, 20 percent of the labor force, or nearly 150 million people, are migrants. Their value added is taxed in the urban areas, whereas their dependents often reside in rural areas of the hinterlands, which are short of fiscal resources to deliver the needed services.

23. Some findings reported in OECD (2005b) point to increasing regional specialization and interregional trade between 1998 and 2003.

24. Demurger (2001) finds that differences in transport and telecommunication infrastructure do affect the growth of individual provinces.

25. China is preparing to list segments of its rail network on domestic and overseas stock markets to raise the resources for expanding the network to 100,000 kilometers by 2020, double tracking half of the network—currently 40 percent is double tracked—and electrifying half of the track, only 30 percent of which is electrified now ("China's Railways" 2005).

damentally a decentralized economic system. This is the stark contrast to the interstate commerce clause of the U.S. constitution, which explicitly prohibits local authorities from undertaking such activities. How to strengthen this capacity at the center is one of the issues that should be addressed. A second regulatory hindrance relates to the entry of and competition among providers of logistics (especially foreign providers) and the latitude granted to large retailers to create nationwide distribution networks (Cheung, Chu, and Penhirin 2002). Retailers such as Wal-Mart have substantially raised productivity and, through their innovations, transformed manufacturing logistics and warehousing in the United States (see Incandela, McLaughlin, and Shi 1999). Progress on both fronts hinges on making changes in regulations and implementing rules in the face of local opposition, as well as having a localized judiciary system that favors local firms in commercial disputes.

Moving to Cities

Managing urbanization to absorb migration and enhance agglomeration effects could dramatically increase the returns to the economy. Past migration—inter- and intra-sectoral—has contributed to growth by raising the productivity of workers, and remittances by migrants have raised household incomes in some of the poorest rural areas. This poverty-reducing, growth bonus will continue to accrue as long as the urban economy continues to generate jobs, as more people will shift from lower-value-adding agricultural employment to industrial and service sector jobs with higher value added. When migration opens up opportunities for the poor, whether in rural areas or in urban centers, and generates a flow of resources to the rural sector via remittances, migration directly lessens poverty.[26]

Should China, therefore, take steps to induce a larger flow of migrants? The evidence suggests that permitting more people to move into urban centers would be in consonance with the Eleventh Plan objectives of achieving balance. By one estimate, dismantling the *hukou* system would reduce the urban-to-rural income differences to a ratio of 2.27 to 1 by

---

26. The level of remittances tends to decrease gradually and eventually stops once migrants permanently settle and bring their family to the urban area. As noted earlier, the poverty rate was 50 percent higher among urban migrants (after remittances) than among permanent urban residents in 2001 (Taylor 2004a). This could be the result largely of migrants' propensity to maximize the remittances sent to their region of origin.

2007 (Hertel and Zhai 2004). Before exploring the policy actions that China might implement, we need to enter a number of caveats.

First, a swelling of migration streams will place heavy burdens on a few coastal provinces and cities that attract migrants. To absorb the migrants without worsening unemployment or aggravating urban poverty, these destinations will have to make large investments in infrastructure, housing, and services and create an environment that stimulates the entry of firms that provide jobs for newcomers. This will be easier for some urban regions than for others and will require building a national fiscal system that generates an adequate level of revenue and effects interprovincial fiscal transfers to achieve a degree of horizontal equity.

Second, a surge in migration can create transitional shortages of housing and services that, if they are not tackled swiftly, could lead to persistent structural problems of poverty and pockets of urban decay. High population density increases the risks from communicable diseases, unless appropriate health systems with the capacity to monitor health conditions and respond quickly to problems are in place. In the major Latin American and South Asian cities, the emergence of slums inadequately supplied with public services has given rise to a host of recalcitrant social ills.

Third, by depleting the population of younger, more educated, and entrepreneurial males—and increasingly females—in rural areas, migration risks eroding agricultural productivity and the development of rural off-farm activities. However, there are as yet few grounds for believing that the rural economy is suffering as a result of migration. The better-educated and better-off members of the farming community are less likely to emigrate in search of the typically menial entry-level jobs in cities. Most migrants are from families that are land poor (DFID 2004). Moreover, migrants generally retain links with their home village and continue to contribute to production activities, directly through labor inputs and indirectly through annual remittances of between Y3,000 and Y4,000 per migrant. Up to a third return to settle and, in some cases, start businesses (Fan 2004b; Murphy 2002).

Each of these and other concerns needs to be weighed carefully, and it might well be that a gradual increase in migration flows—if such calibration is feasible—is the better strategy. This is assuming that urban centers use the time gained to prepare for a substantial increase in population. Such advance planning has been the exception rather than the rule, but it is an objective that the Eleventh Plan could forcefully implement.

Assuming that migration is treated as one of the principal means of both supporting industrial growth and achieving balanced development, reforming the *hukou* and rural land markets could facilitate the flow of migrants, minimize the disruptions they might cause, and increase the likelihood that migration could help to meet national objectives.

Migration Policy and Reform of the *Hukou* System

The *hukou* system was introduced in the late 1950s as a major instrument of migration control.[27] In recent years, it has been relaxed to give more flexibility to labor movements. The changes introduced include the granting of "self-supplied food grain" *hukou* in 1984, the ability to obtain a "temporary residence permit" in 1985, and the issuance of national identity cards in 1985. All these measures have made it easier for rural migrants to seek work in urban areas on a temporary basis (Fan 2004b).

Beginning in the late 1980s, many urban governments started to sell *hukou* to potential migrants meeting specified criteria, which varied among cities. Restrictions on rural to urban migration were further eased after 1992. Larger cities such as Shanghai and Shenzhen started to offer the so-called "blue stamp" *hukou* at a cost to each migrant with desired skills (Fan 2004b). In 2001 the State Council approved further changes to the *hukou* system based on the 1997 pilot program. These changes enabled migrants with stable incomes and legal residence in an urban area to obtain local *hukou* in small towns and cities (Fan 2004b).

Although the State Council issued guidelines in 1998 to relax the *hukou* requirements in large cities, the implementation and adoption of the guidelines varied widely among cities. Some cities, such as Shijiazhuang, granted 450,000 new *hukou* between August 2001 and

---

27. The key aspects of the hukou system are the location and classification of hukou as either agricultural or nonagricultural. A citizen with agricultural hukou has access to farmland, while a citizen with nonagricultural hukou has access to jobs, housing, and state-sponsored benefits. Urban hukou refers to a hukou with an urban location and a nonagricultural classification (Fan 2004b). Possession of the right hukou is necessary for an individual to receive social welfare and public services, such as health and education, from municipal governments (Tan 2004). In effect, holders of urban hukou are provided with an "iron rice bowl" of lifetime employment, health care, housing, and pension benefits (Park 2004), a costly commitment, which is why rural-urban migration is strictly controlled (Fan 2004b). As a result, the domestic labor market is fragmented, although the relaxation of the hukou system in recent years has reduced the degree of fragmentation (Tan 2004). Tan (2004) finds that the variation in the marginal product of labor declined from 0.45 in 1978 to 0.29 in 1996, with the bulk of variation due to rural-urban labor market fragmentation.

June 2003, and other large and medium cities, such as Nanjing, Xi'an, and Zhuhai, eased their *hukou* criteria considerably. The larger cities, such as Beijing, Guangzhou, and Shanghai, however, have resisted further relaxation of *hukou*, citing concerns about pressure on services and the appearance of shanty towns ("China: 'hukou' System" 2006). These cities are focusing more on attracting highly skilled workers and investors (Fan 2004b).

In 2003 the State Council eliminated restrictions on migrants' employment opportunities,[28] the aim being to complete the *hukou* reform in the large cities by eliminating fees for temporary residency (Park 2004) and replacing the dualistic registration system with a unified registration system by 2006 (Fan 2004b). These are important steps, but they stop short of dismantling the *hukou*. Eliminating the barriers that local authorities enforce with varying degrees of severity is desirable both to promote productivity and to achieve greater equity.

It is estimated that an effective removal of the *hukou* system could decrease the Gini coefficient to 0.27, 0.28, and 0.29 for within-urban inequality, within-rural inequality, and inequality overall, respectively (Whalley and Zhang 2004). Currently, within-urban inequality is 0.32, within-rural inequality is 0.35, and inequality overall is 0.46. Such a step would require addressing *hukou*-related benefits and the pace of change. The first concerns the entitlement associated with the *hukou* system; the second relates to the speed at which policy changes are implemented.

Regardless of how the reforms are implemented, migration from the central-western region to the eastern region in pursuit of better economic opportunities will be large. Although it is hard to predict how many people will be on the move, one estimate puts the number at 45 percent of the rural population (Whalley and Zhang 2004). Opinion remains divided on whether the poorest rural inhabitants, many of whom are from ethnic minorities, will join the migrant stream, as it is harder for them to find jobs and to assimilate with the Han majority in urban areas (DFID 2004).

The policy toward farm leasehold rights will be an important factor influencing permanent as against temporary migration. At present, the village collective owns farmland and leases it to households for 30 years. The allocations are adjusted periodically at the discretion of the village

---

28. In the late 1990s, many cities restricted the eligibility of migrants to certain kinds of jobs (Park 2004).

leaders, based on the changing circumstances of households (an increase or reduction in size), commercial opportunities sought after by village officials, and whether or not households are adequately using the land (Krusekopf 2002; Yang 1997). Although households have use rights, these are poorly defined. Moreover, even though the government permits households to transfer their leases to others, thereby encouraging a market for land, village authorities have generally resisted such transactions, opting for administrative allocation that can be arbitrary and is governed by evolving opportunities. The net result of the prevailing arrangement is that households lacking an adequate social safety net in the rural areas and not anticipating that they will be provided with such a net if they migrate to the cities not only hold onto their leased farmland but also continue cultivating it for purposes of insurance. For this reason, men migrate to the cities, only to return periodically, and much of the burden of farming falls on women. This practice also results in the persistent fragmentation of farmland into tiny parcels, which can depress productivity.

Policies that encourage the development of markets for trading land leases would be advantageous in at least three respects.[29] First, they would permit permanent migrants to dispose of their leasehold at a fair price and move with their family to urban areas. Second, such sales would allow for the consolidation of land into more viable farms. And third, outmigration and land consolidation could lead to a rise in average household incomes and reverse the feminization of farming (Ho and Lin 2003; Wu, Liu, and Davis 2005). The spread of what are still relatively scattered and embryonic land markets could, however, accelerate the transfer of workers to cities and increase the need for better urban safety nets for the newcomers. Hertel and Zhai (2004) estimate that well-functioning land markets would increase the out-migration from agriculture by an additional 10 million persons through 2007. In addition to changes in land policy, the establishment of a rural safety net would encourage the trading of land use rights and migration, as land would no longer function as a substitute for a safety net. Furthermore, formalizing land rights would permit farmers to mortgage land to raise capital for investment in agriculture and rural industry alike.

The *hukou* serves two functions: first is to register residence for informational purposes. This function does not need to change, although the

---

29. The lack of health and education benefits is particularly disadvantageous for migrants. For example, only 10 percent of migrant women can afford to deliver their babies in a hospital, which raises the maternal mortality rate for migrants (Taylor 2004a).

issuance of the national identity card is making the *hukou* registration redundant. A much more difficult decision concerns entitlements, the second function of the urban *hukou* system. One approach would be to eliminate or reduce entitlements, such as entitlement to housing, education, and health, for all urban residents. The other would be to retain the entitlements and extend them to migrants on arrival to cities. The choice made will affect the pattern and decision of future migrants. For instance, if all entitlements are retained and the appropriate *hukou* is given to migrants on arrival, migrants may be more willing to abandon their farmland and move the whole family permanently to an urban area (Fan 2004a).[30]

Eliminating the urban entitlements would reduce the fiscal costs for cities and the flow of migrants (since the perceived benefit would be smaller and the risks higher). The migrants may retain their ties to local communities by leaving some family members behind in case they need to return, thus potentially avoiding the development of slums in cities. Eventually, though, national and subnational governments must come to terms with the need for a stronger social safety net for current residents as well as for newcomers to the cities. This would mean expanding the *dibao* (the minimum living standards scheme), which presently is paid only to 21 million urban residents with the *hukou*, while raising the poverty threshold, which is set at the bare minimum income level (DFID 2004). Social safety net spending is lower in China than in the Organisation for Economic Co-operation and Development (OECD) countries. China only spent 0.2 percent of GDP on *dibao* in 2002 (World Bank 2003d).[31] Currently, the eligibility and benefit levels of *dibao* vary considerably across municipalities, and, as a first step, this needs to be unified to provide consistent benefits. The financing responsibility of *dibao* could also be made more transparent, and a system of monitoring and evaluation could be introduced to assess the policy impact (World Bank 2003d).

---

30. The circulatory pattern of migration seen in China reflects the lack of ownership of farmland by peasants, similar to the situation in Mexico. Thus migrants tend to leave a family member behind to tend their farmland while they are away. This helps to maintain the family and social ties with the rural community (Fan 2004a). However, once the entitlements are extended to migrants, it is likely that the entire family will choose to migrate, severing the tie with the rural community.

31. The OECD average is 2.6 percent of GDP, although Japan, Korea, and the United States spend only 0.5 percent, 0.7 percent, and 0.7 percent of GDP, respectively (World Bank 2003d).

Irrespective of how quickly the government acts to modify the social safety net, essential public services, such as basic education, basic public health, and urban infrastructure, will need to be augmented substantially to accommodate the new arrivals and be made available to migrants without discrimination. By making social services available to migrants on the same basis as to urban residents, municipalities could limit the poverty and deprivation experienced by migrants. Alternatively, the services could be provided at subsidized rates. Irrespective of how it is done, the issues posed by urban services and social security for urban residents and migrants must be resolved over the near term.

Two factors are likely to influence the speed of reform. On the benefit side, the economy as a whole will derive static efficiency gains from a better allocation of factors and future agglomeration effects. Against these benefits, national and subnational governments must weigh the fiscal, financial, and social costs of migration for cities, especially when their infrastructure and social policies are not ready to accommodate a surge in migration. Moreover, dismantling the remaining checks on migration (including the scope for leasing rural land) is likely to lead to less-informed migration decisions, with the potential for simply moving rural poverty to urban areas. With slower reform, information on the actual conditions (economic and social) in the host cities can be transmitted back to sending provinces, enabling rural communities and potential migrants to prepare for the exodus (Fan 2004a).

The Chinese government relaxed the *hukou* system in smaller cities first in order to contain the congestion costs associated with a significantly greater influx of migrants to large cities. However, this could lead to wasteful investment in smaller cities if these migrants do not move to cities where the government expects them to go (Park 2004). Moreover, the agglomeration effects discussed earlier might not be realized.

The final and critical stage of *hukou* system reform must be coordinated with other actions if it is to contribute both to the growth of the economy and to the reduction of inequality between regions and sectors. Governments need to reappraise their role with respect to taxation and the provision of services (for example, how much of the services, entitlements, and a safety net should be provided by the public sector, at what rates, and subject to which criteria). In addition, there may be a need to reallocate fiscal resources among different levels of government to better accommodate the redistribution of the population from rural to urban counties.

National Innovation System, Information Technology, and FDI

A close second to intersectoral transfer of factors is the effect of the inno-vation system on long-run total factor productivity and competitiveness. As Woetzel (2003) and many others have observed, China's industrial competitiveness cannot rest on low costs alone; in today's markets, rou-tinizing innovation is a necessary objective for firms, and in the industri-al economies it is becoming the determinant of TFP (Baumol 2002; Yusuf and others 2003).

China has recognized the role of innovation for some time, and, in 1999, following the National Technological Innovation Conference in Beijing, the government began assembling a "national innovation system." The purpose of this system is to link reforms with science and technology development, education, and innovation (Sun 2002). In taking this step, the government embraced a systems approach that acknowledges the part played by enterprises (public and private), technology markets, and denser linkages between the producers and the users of innovations. The new strategy has led to the transfer of government laboratories to state-owned enterprises, with half of the more than 22,000 R&D laboratories being transferred to state-owned enterprises by 1999 (see table 3.12). As a con-sequence of this strategy, the share of enterprises in total R&D expendi-ture is rising. Other developments include incentives for research institutes to commercialize their findings and to encourage start-up firms that draw on the expertise of the research centers and on new sources of venture capital from government and private funds (Sun 2002).[32] The efforts to commercialize technology have been backed by attempts to enforce intel-lectual property rights more stringently and by the emergence of numer-ous technology-trading organizations (260,000 in 1998). The government

Table 3.12. R&D Expenditure in China, by Sector, 1999–2002

percent

Sector	1999	2000	2001	2002	2003
R&D institutes	33.4	28.8	27.7	27.3	27.1
Universities	8.1	8.6	9.8	10.1	10.5
Industries	55.4	60.0	60.4	61.2	60.1
Others	3.1	2.6	2.1	1.4	1.3

Source: OECD 2005a.

---

32. A detailed summary of the fiscal incentives for innovation is contained in Yusuf, Wang, and Nabeshima (2005).

is also encouraging the development of information technology and telecommunications and has poured billions into building a modern ICT (information and communications technology) infrastructure.

These actions are reflected in much higher expenditures on R&D (China is now ranked third in the world, after the United States and Japan)[33] and an increase in the number of scientists and engineers engaged in research (1 million in 2004). In a number of respects, however, the innovation system still needs strengthening. Between 1995 and 2003, China's share of patents applied for or approved by the U.S. Patent and Trademark Office or the European Patent Office were only 0.3 percent of the total (OECD 2004a). Furthermore, most of the domestic patent applications are for utility (40 percent) and external design patents (36 percent; see table 3.13), although the share of invention patents has increased: from 14 to 24 percent between 1996 and 2004 (Cheung and Lin 2004; "State Intellectual Property Office of China" 2005. In contrast, patent applications by foreign residents are highly concentrated in invention patents (86 percent in 2004), compared with 12 percent for external design patents and only 1 percent for utility patents (Cheung and Lin 2004; "State Intellectual Property Office of China" 2005.

The bulk of the research continues to be conducted by institutes of the state and is financed by government state laboratories, which absorbed two-thirds of science and technology personnel in 1999. Meanwhile, universities conduct relatively little research and still command a modest fraction of R&D funding. Neither they nor research institutes conduct much basic research (Judson 2006). In fact, the share of basic research has declined and was just 5.7 percent of total R&D expenditure in 2002, well below that of comparators although efforts are ongoing to increase basic research in six areas through the 97-3 program (see table 3.14). The consequence of this is that only one physicist was awarded China's Natural Science Award during 2001–3; China is ranked eighth in the Science Citation Index,[34] and papers published in leading science journals such as Science and Nature are on paleontology and geology (Cao 2004).

In spite of the efforts made, the links between research entities and firms remain sparse, and few innovations are being commercialized. Even the laboratories transferred to state-owned enterprises have difficulty

---

33. China spent $103 billion in PPP-adjusted dollars in 2004, the United States spent $313 billion, and Japan spent $113 billion (OECD 2005a). By 2020, China plans to raise spending on R&D to 2.5 percent of GDP.

34. However, this is a vast improvement over the twenty-sixth ranking in 1985.

Table 3.13. Patent Applications Submitted by Domestic and Foreign Residents in China, by Type of Patent, 1996, 1998, and 2000

Type of patent	1996	1998	2000	2002	2004
Domestic applications					
Number of applications	82,207	96,233	140,339	205,544	278,943
Type of patent (percent of total)					
Invention	13.95	14.26	18.06	19.4	23.6
Utility model	60.02	53.22	48.78	44.8	40.0
External design	26.03	32.51	33.16	35.8	36.4
Overseas applications					
Number of applications	20,528	25,756	30,343	47,087	74,864
Type of patent (percent of total)					
Invention	83.04	86.33	87.01	85.9	86.0
Utility model	1.28	0.69	1.17	2.1	1.7
External design	15.18	12.99	11.82	12.1	12.4

Source: Cheung and Lin 2004; "State Intellectual Property Office of China" 2005

Table 3.14. Basic Research Expenditure as a Share of Total R&D Expenditure in China and Other Countries, Various Years

Country and year	Percent of total
Switzerland, 1998	27.90
Australia, 1998	26.60
Italy, 1998	22.20
France, 1999	24.40
Czech Republic, 2000	36.60
United States, 1997	18.10
Singapore, 1993	16.10
Korea, Rep. of, 1994	14.00
Japan. 1999	12.30
China, 2002	5.70

Source: National Bureau of Statistics of China and Ministry of Science and Technology 2002, pp. 250–1; 2003, pp. 438–9; Yusuf, Wang, and Nabeshima 2005.

making their mark because they frequently lack the incentives to inno-vate. In those instances where research centers have spun off new enter-prises, they tend to assert their control, which hampers development of the new firms. On the whole, innovative activity among state-owned enterprises and privately owned firms is weak, and this is compounded by the slowness with which firms have moved to embrace information tech-nology and the relatively weak enforcement afforded to intellectual prop-erty by the legal system (Yusuf and Evenett 2002).

A number of steps could raise the tempo of innovative activity.

First, state-owned enterprises, which control a large share of the public sector's science and technology assets, should have the autonomy and the incentives to engage more actively in innovation, not just product and process innovation, but also innovation in organizational structure and business models. This is most likely to be achieved through privatization of at least the largest manufacturing enterprises with the greatest R&D capability. This also applies to spin-offs. We return to this below.

Second, enterprises should be encouraged to embrace information technology, which in the industrial countries is associated with more rapid innovation in product, process, and design areas.[35] This can be achieved through the assistance of business associations in setting up B2B (business-to-business) exchanges, assistance particularly to smaller businesses provided by technical institutes, investment in broadband infrastructure, and competitive pricing of telecommunication services.[36]

Third, select universities should be induced to place greater emphasis on research and be able to obtain the financing needed to acquire essential lab equipment and journals (Cao 2004). This would improve the quality of their graduates and pave the way for fruitful collaboration with industry. The problems universities face in transferring innovations to firms—which often have difficulty adapting the innovation for commercial purposes—could be reduced by strengthening and multiplying intermediary institutions, as exist in Germany, Italy, and Japan, that provide technical assistance to small firms to seek out, acquire, assimilate, and debug new technologies (Kodama and Suzuki 2005).

Fourth, China must continue to try to harness more effectively the potential for transferring technology that resides in FDI. This is being tapped, but by no means fully. We discuss the possibilities below.

A wealth of evidence suggests that the private returns from R&D leading to innovation can average 28 percent, overshadowing the returns from other investments, and that the social benefits are even higher (Wieser 2005). Innovating across a broad range of facilities, in turn, feeds TFP. Hence routinizing innovation across a spectrum of businesses is vital to growth. This, in turn, calls for an innovation system that is an

---

35. This is all the more important since, in 2006, China attained the largest Internet population in the world: more than 150 million subscribers ("Net's Second Superpower" 2004).

36. Telecom producers such as Huawei are investing heavily in R&D, are able to offer state-of-the-art equipment for optical, fixed, and mobile communications, and can provide network operators with turnkey solutions plus financing (Saha 2004).

intersection of incentives, institutions, and resources, frequently adjusted so as to stay abreast of a changing business environment and international best practice. Among the policy instruments available to the government are fiscal incentives for firms (local and foreign) to conduct R&D.[37] These are usually reinforced by direct government grants for technology development and purchase contracts that defray some of the costs of new product development. The states' efforts to define and enforce intellectual property rights through the legal system are crucial for promoting innovation in myriad high-tech industries. Both intellectual property and legal institutions are in need of strengthening (Hufbauer and Wong 2004). Governments also are the prime movers when it comes to sustaining research universities and research institutes that generate fresh ideas as well as potentially commercializable technologies. And government initiatives induce university business linkages and provide the institutional infrastructure for assigning as well as protecting property rights.

The government's role is undoubtedly substantial, but firms remain the lynchpin of the innovation system. A firm's management, strategy, and business model fundamentally fixes the centrality of innovation. In the United States, firms responsible for process innovations, such as Dell and Wal-Mart, have contributed hugely to productivity growth. So have product innovators, such as Intel, Texas Instruments, and the pharmaceutical companies. The same goes for Japanese companies, such as Canon and Toyota. In China, companies such as Changhong Electric, Haier, Huawei, TCL, and ZTE are learning to harness technology and to compete on the basis of innovation.

The most enterprising companies in China share a number of characteristics. They are either foreign joint ventures or reformed state-owned enterprises whose management enjoys a large degree of autonomy. They are engaged in alliances and partnerships so as to leverage the strengths of other firms, and they are constantly alert to the opportunities for technology transfer from new start-ups and myriad other channels. Most firms also find that a choice urban location and linkages with universities are necessities because in-house research is generally developmental and often narrowly specialized. Association with universities permits access to a wider menu of potential technological choices, in particular where partner universities are engaged in basic research.

---

37. See Yusuf, Wang, and Nabeshima (2005). This is already generous, especially in the technology development zones.

The innovation system thus threads together technology policies with skill development in urban centers, the building of market institutions, and private ownership. Individually, each can contribute modestly to economic performance; together their impact is vastly greater.[38]

Another role for the innovation system that relates to China's growing need for energy, raw materials, and water concerns food security. Pricing policies, enforcement of conservation rules, and efficient production practices, among others, will moderate the growth of demand. But in China, as in other OECD countries, the consumption of energy, water, and other raw materials per unit of GDP and the productivity of agriculture will be managed, in large part, through technological advances. For instance, advances in agricultural biotechnology will determine agricultural growth (Huang and others 2004), hybrid automobile and fuel cell technologies will affect the use of hydrocarbon energy, while miniaturization and the greater use of lightweight composites will moderate the demand for metals. New irrigation techniques can reduce water inputs and losses, and pollution controls can improve water quality. These are just a few examples. Technological advancement can have widespread ramifications, and the success of China's strategy for sustainable growth hinges on it.

FDI in China

Foreign direct investment is one of the major channels for technology transfer.[39] There are various ways in which FDI can contribute to the development of technological capabilities in a host country: new technology embedded in equipment and processes, demonstration effects, the circulation of managers and workers, competitive pressures, and technological links between foreign firms and their suppliers and subsidiaries.

Urban centers in Fujian, Guangdong, Jiangsu, and Shanghai absorb more than 50 percent of all FDI, benefiting from their coastal location, fewer regulatory impediments, and close proximity to two of the biggest investors: Hong Kong, China, and Taiwan, China (Hsiao and Hsiao 2004; Ng and Tuan 2003). Much of investment in Guangdong is concentrated in special economic zones and other cities in the Pearl River Delta with-

---

38. On how privatization can contribute to industrial productivity, see Yusuf, Nabeshima, and Perkins (2005). And on the "new" breed of reformed Chinese firms, see Yusuf and Nabeshima (2006).

39. See Saggi (2002) for an extensive review of the links between FDI and technology transfer; see Nabeshima (2004) for a review of the literature on technology transfer.

in 200 kilometers of Hong Kong, China (Ng and Tuan 2003).[40] The location of FDI is closely keyed to the originating host economy. Capital from Hong Kong (China) flows mainly to Shenzhen; from Taiwan (China) to Dongguan, Xiamen, and the urban region centered on Shanghai; from Japan and Korea to Liaoning and Shandong; and from the European Union and the United States to Beijing, Guangdong, Shanghai, and Tianjing, reflecting proximity and cultural and linguistic ties (Hsiao and Hsiao 2004). This geographic distribution of FDI is building technological capability and augmenting the agglomeration effects of the coastal metropolitan region.[41]

What economic benefits stem from FDI in China?[42] There are three broad measures that one can use: productivity, export performance, and innovation. The research on productivity—measured by TFP—so far points to positive spillover effects from FDI, although the findings vary (Lim 2001). For instance, while some studies point to horizontal spillover, others find vertical spillovers to be a more important source of technology transfer, consistent with the findings from Indonesia (Blalock and Gertler 2003).[43] Hence joint ventures in which the foreign investor has a major share are a more effective vehicle for transferring technology. Recent research by Yusuf, Nabeshima, and Perkins (2005) using enterprise data validates this finding.

With respect to performance, about 57 percent of Chinese exports are generated by joint ventures and wholly owned foreign subsidiaries (Hsiao and Hsiao 2004; Zhu 2005).[44] Many empirical studies point to

---

40. Guangdong alone accounts for one-third of FDI and, by 2003, had attracted $140 billion ("Province Achieves" 2004).

41. While coastal provinces were able to take advantage of export-oriented FDI, it did not offer any growth linkages to inland provinces, since these operations are highly dependent on imported materials for their processing trade. This has exacerbated inequality among regions (Fu 2004).

42. In this section, we focus on the benefits arising from FDI in manufacturing industries. FDI in services, especially financial services, can have similar positive effects, such as improved efficiency and greater capacity to avoid crises (Goldberg 2004).

43. See other studies on the United Kingdom (Haskel, Pereira, and Slaughter 2002) and the United States (Keller and Yeaple 2003). R&D and firm size have positive effects on the level of TFP (Liu and Wang 2003). See also a study on Latvia, where firms supplying multinational companies tend to receive technical assistance much more frequently (FIAS 2003), and on Lithuania (Javorcik 2004).

44. Whether such high export ratios signal the improvement in technological capability among Chinese firms is questionable. Foreign firms may be bringing in the technology to enable firms to export, or they may be purchasing firms capable of exporting but unable to initiate the move due to lack of resources (mainly financial resources to

links stemming from FDI to exports and vice versa (Liu, Wang, and Wei 2001; Zhang and Felmingham 2001; Zhang and Song 2001). In fact, some studies suggest that exports signal the way to investment in China's central provinces (Zhang and Felmingham 2001). As multinational companies begin to focus more on the domestic market, there will be a greater readiness to locate in major urban centers in the interior of the country, depending on the reduction in freight and transaction costs ("Go West" 2005). Chongqing, Shaanxi, and Sichuan, in particular, are making determined efforts to woo foreign investors through incentives, streamlined regulations, and investment in infrastructure, but large gaps in manufacturing capability still need to be narrowed ("Interior Has Strategic" 2004).

Foreign firms are investing in China primarily to take advantage of low labor costs,[45] but a secondary attraction is the opportunity to transfer some R&D to China, mainly to a few metropolitan centers with a base of strong skills.[46] In addition, smaller foreign suppliers to the large multinational companies move in to serve their clients and to exploit the clustering and agglomeration effects, especially in the coastal cities (Ng and Tuan 2003).[47] Given that much investment in China is of relatively small scale, clustering behavior and the gains from such association are considerable. FDI, therefore, contributes to the innovative capability of Chinese firms, measured by the increase in patent applications (design, invention, and utility) submitted by domestic residents. Using provincial data from 1995 to 2000, Cheung and Lin (2004) show that applications for external design patents increased dramatically following FDI (elastic-

---

private firms) and differential treatment accorded to foreign and domestic private enterprises (Huang 2001b; Huang and Di 2004). As a result, they disguise themselves as "foreign" firms by routing financing through the Virgin Islands and the Cayman Islands, which account for 13 percent of FDI (Hsiao and Hsiao 2004); large flows also come from Hong Kong (China), some of which are speculated to be "round-tripping."

45. See Hsiao and Hsiao (2004). Because of this, low-skilled workers in source countries tend to be adversely affected, while higher-skilled workers gain through further specialization in the source countries (Chen and Ku 2003). This should be viewed in relation to the findings of Cheng and Kwan (2000), who note that location decisions by multinational companies between 1985 and 1995 were influenced by the income per capita of provinces, infrastructure provision, and the status of special economic zones and other preferential zones for foreign direct investment.

46. China is becoming an attractive location for multinational companies wanting to offshore their R&D facilities because of China's rising supply of science and technology skills and the relatively low cost of workers with them (UNCTAD 2005).

47. Overall, 87 percent of FDI is in the coastal areas, which also produce 93 percent of manufactured exports ("Interior Has Strategic" 2004).

ity of 0.5), pointing to the "demonstration" effect of FDI. But, so far, the spillovers from FDI to utility patents are hard to detect (Cheung and Lin 2004).

Promoting FDI

The rate of return on FDI in China (5.9 percent) between 1999 and 2002 was much lower than the world average of 6.5 percent and lower than that of Hong Kong, China (12.5 percent), Malaysia (12.3 percent), and the Philippines (7.3 percent)(Hsiao and Hsiao 2004).[48] To increase returns, to sustain or even enlarge the flow of FDI, and to shift more of it into higher-tech industries, seven sets of policy initiatives should be considered.[49]

First is the continuing liberalization of the economy and integration of markets (Lim 2001). The second involves increasing the supply of skilled workers and, in particular, improving their quality. Third is raising the caliber of key universities and strengthening their research orientation so as to attract more FDI in higher-level research and to motivate collaborative alliances with multinational companies and foreign research centers. Fourth are legal and enforcement measures to help secure intellectual property rights.[50] Fifth is the strengthening of institutions and practices that result in a stable and predictable policy environment and contracting arrangements enforced by a higher-quality, more independent judiciary. Sixth is improving logistics that facilitate the seamlessly integrated multimodal transport of goods within the country, encouraging FDI in the central region, and reducing costs, which can amount to as much as 20 percent of the price of a product. This could be assisted by measures to improve policy formulation and investment planning for the transport sector as a whole, either by strengthening the National Development and Reform Commission or by merging the Ministry of Commerce and the Ministry of Railways into a comprehensive Ministry of Transport, after separating the railway enterprise from the government's regulatory functions. Horizontal consultation and coordination across branches of

---

48. Earnings of U.S. companies from China in 2003 were $8.2 billion as against $7.1 billion from Australia, $8.9 billion from Taiwan (China) and Korea, and $14.3 billion from Mexico ("Cut-Throat Competition" 2004).
49. China received a quarter of all FDI to developing countries over the past decade and is aiming to attract 30 percent in the next 10 years (Zhu 2005).
50. Evidence from Eastern Europe points to the importance of protecting intellectual property rights for attracting technology-intensive FDI (Smarzynska Javorcik 2004).

government (for example, on subjects such as road safety and truck over-loading) would reinforce this process.

The seventh and final policy initiative concerns the quality of the urban environment. FDI in high-tech and knowledge-intensive activities is closely associated with skilled workers who attach importance to living conditions and lifestyle choices. Thus attracting FDI into advanced electronics or biotech industries, for example, is synonymous with attracting knowledge workers and their families to urban locations. Municipalities in Europe and the United States have discovered that talented and highly paid knowledge workers are drawn to cities with an abundance of social, housing, cultural, and recreational amenities, combined with environmental quality and a low incidence of crime. U.S. cities such as Austin, San Diego, San Francisco, Minneapolis, and others have made determined efforts to create a physical and social ambience conducive to the growth of high-tech industries, with considerable success. In East Asia, Singapore is consciously pursuing such a strategy in an effort to attract the "star researchers" who can generate the technological "buzz" and catalyze the emergence of high-tech clusters in areas such as biotechnology (Yusuf and Nabeshima 2005). And the importance of urban amenities for the next stage of industrial development is galvanizing other Asian cities, such as Bangalore and Seoul, to focus on lifestyle choices (Florida 2000).

The use of investment incentives, especially fiscal incentives, should be selective and keep a close eye on the benefits of tax expenditures. First, according to many surveys of managers of multinational companies, fiscal incentives are typically given lower priority than other factors, such as wage costs, market potential, investment risks, and exit costs—related to labor regulations, for example (Görg 2005; Wells and others 2001).[51] In spite of this, many countries offer a plethora of investment incentives. In fact, few countries exercise restraint, even though the empirical evidence on the effectiveness of fiscal incentives in attracting FDI is mixed at best (Blomstrom and Kokko 2003; Lim 2001). The consensus seems to be that the firms most likely to respond to fiscal incentives are banks, insurance companies, and companies related to the Internet and engaged in relative-

---

51. However, fiscal incentives can be useful tools if two locations offer similar advantages to multinational companies. For instance, two cities competing with each other for FDI within a country may find it necessary to offer fiscal incentives to affect the location decision. Whether this policy is cost-effective is hard to say (Wells and others 2001). Still, the overall results from the studies by Held and others (1999), Hines (1996), and Hubert and Pain (2002) on FDI in the European Union and the United States suggest that fiscal incentives were a factor in the FDI of multinational companies.

ly footloose activities associated with export-oriented processing (Blomstrom and Kokko 2003; Morisset 2003).[52]

Second, the consensus is that the cost of incentives exceeds the benefits accruing from FDI spillovers.[53] The reasons are that the costs of incentives, which typically are given in the form of tax concessions (or outright tax exemptions), are hard to assess. Equally difficult to measure are the spillover benefits, which are also spread over time, although the physical investment and generation of local employment are realized in a short span of time. Because of this mismatch in the timing of costs and benefits as well as the difficulties in measurement, investment incentives are generally excessive (Blomstrom and Kokko 2003).[54] The end result typically is the transfer of wealth from the host country to the multinational company or, worse, to the government that hosts the multinational company's headquarters. This is particularly so if the main purpose of FDI is "market seeking."

As is likely, the future flow of FDI to China will increasingly serve the vast domestic market. Integration of the domestic market and improvement of the urban business environment would be the most effective means of attracting foreign investment. Providing additional incentives would be more akin to a pure wealth transfer.

State-Owned Enterprise and Banking Sector Reforms

The ownership reform of state-owned enterprises and the banking system can powerfully reinforce the impact of urbanization, innovation, and IT use on growth. There are a number of reasons why privatizing state-owned manufacturing industries and reforming banking system ownership should be at the top of the reform agenda.

First, the experience in China thus far and around the world is that privatization—and even coporatization in the Chinese case—is associated with substantial improvements in productivity and return on assets (Yusuf, Nabeshima, and Perkins 2005; OECD 2005b.

Second, state-owned enterprises, with the support of banks, still absorb

---

52. For instance, Motorola invested in Scotland, employing 3,000 workers in 1991 and receiving $51 million as part of the incentives. It closed the factory in 2001, repaying $17 million. Similarly, Siemens opened a factory in northern England in 1996, only to close it 18 months later (Haskel, Pereira, and Slaughter 2002).
53. See, for instance, Haskel, Pereira, and Slaughter (2002).
54. This is similar to trade protection. Similarly, specific policies tend to breed corruption (Blomstrom and Kokko 2003).

up to two-thirds of all credit, even though the share of state-owned enterprises in industrial GDP has declined to one-fifth.[55] Indeed, this results in a disproportionate flow of credit to provinces with the largest concentration of state-owned enterprises (Honohan 2004). These provinces are neither the poorest nor necessarily the ones with the highest growth potential. Research shows that state-owned enterprises are the least-productive form of enterprise, well behind joint ventures, collectives, and private firms, and that up to a third make operating losses.[56] State-owned enterprises not only absorb a large volume of resources and, in the process, add to the overhang of excess capacity in many manufacturing subsectors but also divert resources from more efficient users and limit the entry of new producers (Wen 2004b). Because the entry of new firms and the exit of failing firms are a source of productivity growth within industrial sectors, industrial policies that limit entry and exit and use the banking system to shore up ailing state firms waste resources, sacrifice productivity growth, weaken the state-owned banking industry, and build up contingent liabilities in the budget.

Third, the presence of excess capacity in the state sector (although not just in the state sector) and of state-owned enterprises that continue producing even while incurring substantial losses places great pressure on other firms. These firms, many of which are more efficient than the state-owned enterprises, must compete on unequal terms and make lower profits or even losses, despite their higher efficiency, because of underbidding by state-owned enterprises. As a consequence, they are unable to finance growth by accumulating resources internally or raising funds in the market. Most Chinese firms have remained small, yet highly diversified to secure cash flow and, partly for that reason, are slow to engage in innovative activity (Steinfeld 2004a).

A fourth reason stems from the relationships between state-owned enterprises and their supervising county or provincial agencies. For these

---

55. See Honohan (2004) and Liu and Wang (2005), who also show that, during the period they studied, high-risk state-owned enterprises were able to raise more funding from banks than lower-risk enterprises. However, smaller-scale surveys suggest that this could be changing, with state-owned enterprises receiving less credit. See also OECD (2005b) on the role of the private sector.

56. See Yusuf, Nabeshima, and Perkins (2005) for a review of the literature on transition economies and the findings of an extensive survey of Chinese firms. Bai, Lu, and Tao (2005) report similar findings. Parker and Kirkpatrick (2005) survey the literature on developing countries and stress the need for effective competition policies and regulatory capacity in order to maximize the gains from privatization. This is also the finding of Konings, van Cayseele, and Warzynski (2005).

agencies, state-owned enterprises are among the main sources of revenue and of employment, and they provide avenues for exercising patronage.[57] Hence local agencies are opposed to relinquishing their ownership and control rights. Moreover, to fatten enterprise profits, they have extended various forms of protection, in the process throwing up barriers to the integration of domestic markets. As noted earlier, the presence of such barriers, and the still underdeveloped logistics infrastructure, prevents China from enjoying the productivity benefits of a vast, integrated, and competitive national market.

A decade and more ago, there may have been grounds for proceeding cautiously with ownership reform of the state sector (see Yusuf, Nabeshima, and Perkins 2005).[58] They are less compelling today and are overshadowed by the economic costs inflicted by the state sector. Having privatized the smaller state-owned enterprises, China has the opportunity, within the course of the Eleventh Plan, to complete a reform that commenced two decades ago (Mohan 2004). There are at least three major facets to this reform.

- *Privatization (or corporatization that gives meaningful autonomy) of most of the remaining manufacturing state-owned enterprises, with the central and subnational governments relinquishing their control rights and allowing full autonomy to management and the board of directors.* In this scenario, the presence of large institutional investors can be a "significant" plus and more effective than many dispersed private shareholders (Mohan 2004).[59] Better corporate governance that gives minority shareholders their voice and disciplines firms by bankruptcy rules, aside from achieving orderly restructuring, will require strong and independent legal institutions, which China currently lacks (Perkins 2004).

- *Full commercialization of the four main state-owned banks by restructuring them, divesting shares to strategic investors, improving governance through*

---

57. The heavy reliance on state-owned enterprises for revenue-generating purposes stems from the lack of fiscal resources at the local level under the current intergovernmental fiscal relations.

58. The evidence summarized in Yusuf, Nabeshima, and Perkins (2005) on the greater efficiency of private enterprises is further buttressed by the findings of a study of Spanish firms, which shows that the productivity of public firms was much lower (González-Páramo and De Cos 2005).

59. Zhang (2004) finds that corporatization has done little to improve the performance of state-owned enterprises.

strong boards of directors, concentrating government ownership in a State Bank Asset Management Organization, and granting full operational autonomy to management within this framework.[60] These steps would build on the ones taken in 2004 to liberalize lending rates and augment capital adequacy ratios ("Banking Sees" 2004). The initial public offerings for two of the four state banks could be a start, in particular if this were to attract strategic investors, which could infuse managerial skills in addition to new capital. Ownership and governance reforms of the smaller banks should be considered as well.

- *Strengthening of the competition laws and empowerment of the regulatory body to effectively oversee the changes that would occur if the loss-making state-owned enterprises were privatized and an active market for capital control were permitted to operate in China.* Undoubtedly, this would unleash a process of rationalization and consolidation of industries. Some of this consolidation should be encouraged because it would lead to larger firms better equipped to conduct R&D and to compete on global markets.[61] Because of the heavy R&D outlay needed for invention patents, domestic applications for these patents are relatively few, reflecting the modest size of even the largest Chinese firms (Nolan 2002).[62] In other cases, consolidation may have to be resisted in the interests of sustaining market competition. The regulator would also be at the forefront of efforts to dismantle provincial industrial policies and barriers to trade.

Undoubtedly, such bold steps would face stiff political resistance, as they have in the past, not the least because they could lead to more layoffs and higher transitional urban unemployment. But if China continues down the politically easier path of gradualism, the country could be

---

60. One concern is the lack of access to credit in the rural areas following ownership reform. However, even with the current system, the four state-owned banks closed 31,000 rural branches in 1999 (Taylor 2004a).
61. On this, see Katz and Shelanski (2004) dealing with U.S. antitrust policy that looks at firm size and innovative activity.
62. By comparison, Indian firms tend on balance to be bigger in size than Chinese firms, even though the domestic markets for various products are much larger in China than in India. For instance, the Hope Group, which is the largest private firm in China, had annual sales of $500 million in 2002. In contrast, India's largest private conglomerate, the Tata Group, had revenues of $14.25 billion in 2003. The largest pharmaceutical company in China, Sanjiu, had sales of $670 million compared with Ranbaxy Laboratories Limited of India, with sales of $2.27 billion (Huang 2001a).

incurring costs much greater than the transitional ones imposed by privatization and would risk compromising some of the growth momentum. The approach to enterprise ownership reform being followed, which leaves control rights of the medium-size and large enterprises with public bureaus, has neither maximized the efficiency gains from corporatization nor reaped the full benefits of market integration. The Eleventh Plan offers an opportunity to complete a process that commenced during the Ninth Plan. But it is a reform that is bound to be resisted, because it would restrict the options of subnational policy makers to orchestrate local industrial development, and because privatization would limit the scope for raising off-budget revenue. Thus enterprise reform needs to be supplemented by changes to the system of fiscal transfers. Such changes are needed, not only because of enterprise reform, but also because of the failure of the current fiscal regime to adequately defray the costs of expenditure assignments and the need for a comprehensive overhaul (Dabla-Norris 2004; Weist 2004). Reform could also be buttressed by more vigorous implementation of active labor market policies so as to hold unemployment in check.

Impact of WTO Accession on the Domestic Economy and Trade Partners

China's integration with the global economy has been accelerated by accession to the WTO. This will have significant and largely positive consequences for the domestic economy through a variety of channels—in particular, trade, FDI, and systems reform. China is expected to gain substantially from the phasing out of the Multi Fibre Agreement, given that 79 percent of China's exports are to nonquota markets (World Bank 2003b, p. 80).[63] Once the Multi Fibre Agreement restrictions were eased in the quota markets, Chinese producers took advantage of expanded opportunities.[64] Exports to the United States grew 57 percent, and exports to the European Union grew 36 percent in the first half of 2005, after the lifting of quotas ("International: China Textile Talks" 2005). However, trade in textiles remains highly protected. Although the Multi

---

63. China's apparel exports account for 45 percent of non-OECD exports (Mallon and Whalley 2004).
64. Colombia is another country that is highly constrained by the Multi Fibre Agreement, with 50 percent of exports to nonquota countries (World Bank 2003b, p. 80). The growth of exports from Bangladesh, Nepal, and Sri Lanka could also be adversely affected (Li 2002).

Fibre Agreement was phased out over a 10-year period ending in 2005, OECD countries can introduce safeguards until 2008. In fact, the European Union and the United States did introduce safeguards to restrict the sale of Chinese imports (Li 2002; Mallon and Whalley 2004).[65] At the same time, as China's trade barriers are dismantled, formerly protected industries will face significant import competition and are likely to grow more slowly. The largest drop in growth is expected in automobiles and auto parts, once tariffs fall in 2006, followed by "other manufactures," metal products, and electronics (Lau 2002; World Bank 2003b, p. 81).[66]

Output of and employment in the agricultural sector are likely to decrease 2–8 percent, except in tobacco, where they will decline 33 percent owing to the high levels of current protection (Anderson, Huang, and Ianchovichina 2004). However, given China's comparative advantage in labor-intensive agricultural products (such as animal husbandry, horticulture, aquaculture, and processed products), production and employment should rise, while production of cotton should remain unaffected (Chang, Fleisher, and Parker 2001).[67]

Farmers in the 3-H basins are likely to shift toward cash crops, especially cotton, with the sown area expanding by up to by 3.5 million mu (one acre is equal to about six mu). Offsetting this would be a decline in the area devoted to wheat of up to 19 million mu. These reductions could lead to a loss of income of around 7 percent (Gunaratnam 2004).

China is committed to liberalizing the services sectors, with little or no corresponding reciprocal concessions from other countries (Mallon and

---

65. China reached an agreement with the United States to restrict the growth of exports to an average of 11 percent a year for 34 categories of apparel and textile products ("As Fleeting as Fashion" 2005). Similarly, the European Union restricted the growth of 10 categories of goods to 8–12 percent ("International: China Textile Talks" 2005).

66. Other estimates suggest that employment will be reduced by 9.66 million (3.6 percent) in the agricultural sector, by 5 million (14.5 percent) in automobiles, and by 6 million (2.5 percent) in machinery and instruments by 2008 (Bhalla and Qiu 2002).

67. Labor-intensive agriculture products accounted for 80 percent of agricultural exports in the late 1990s (Huang, Rozelle, and Chang 2003). The cotton market was deregulated in 1999, allowing farmers to sell all of their harvest in the market, instead of selling a fixed quantity to the government at set prices. Since then, the price of cotton has been rising, and investment in cotton production increased 74 percent in one year, expanding the area planted by 12 percent in 2004, following a 22 percent expansion in 2003 ("Cotton in China" 2004). China still lacks a futures market for cotton. On June 1, 2004, a small-scale futures market for cotton was opened in Zhengzhou, although foreigners are not allowed to participate ("Cotton in China" 2004).

Whalley 2004).[68] In banking, all geographic restrictions on licenses are to be eliminated, with national treatment spanning all types of renminbi and foreign currency businesses (Mallon and Whalley 2004).[69] Such liberalization could lead to gains of as much as 25 percent of GDP (Whalley 2003)[70] if, at the same time, state-owned enterprises are subjected to hard-budget constraints, making state-owned enterprise reform all the more urgent. A large gap exists between the agreed terms, the current practice, and the steps toward banking sector liberalization recently instituted. Therefore, the government will have to take decisive action in order to complete the liberalization by 2007 (Whalley 2003). The government has been encouraging investments by foreign firms into local banks but still prefers to limit them as minority shareholders. The proposed investment by Temasek Holdings of Singapore in the Bank of China is being met with some resistance, and it is highly likely that the China Banking Regulatory Commission will ask for a smaller investment by Temasek ("China Backs" 2005).

China's accession to the WTO is likely to have relatively minimal consequences for other countries, with the exception of those in the South Asian region, which will face severe competition in the garment and textile industries (Yang 2003). Other countries, especially the advanced economies in East Asia, stand to gain substantially from China's accession (Eichengreen, Rhee, and Tong 2004),[71] although further development of the regional division of labor is likely and the light manufactured exports of the middle-income Southeast Asian countries will face stiff competition from Chinese producers (Eichengreen, Rhee, and Tong 2004; McKibbin and Woo 2003; Rumbaugh and Blancher 2003).[72] In 1998, 27 percent of China's imports were intermediate inputs used by the export

---

68. From 2002 to 2007, China is to open its markets fully for distribution, telecommunications, financial services, professional business and computer services, motion pictures, environmental services, accounting, law, architecture, construction, and tourism (Lardy 2002; Whalley 2003).

69. Many foreign banks can only conduct local currency business in Pudong and Shenzen and are allowed to take minority shareholder stakes in local banks (Whalley 2003).

70. Although limited, foreign firms already had 191 offices and subsidiaries in 23 cities in 2000 (Whalley 2003), and by the end of October 2005, the China Banking Regulatory Commission had approved investments by 19 foreign institutions in 16 local banks ("China Backs" 2005).

71. Many economies do not share China's mix of export products, the exceptions being Thailand and countries in South Asia (Shafaeddin 2002).

72. Currently, China's manufacturers of many consumer products are engaged in unsophisticated assembly operations ("China: Trade Boom" 2004).

industries (Shafaeddin 2002).[73] More than 50 percent of China's imports come from East Asia (see table 3.15). At this stage, the pattern of trade favors ASEAN, Japan, and Korea.[74] Whether this balance persists will depend on the degree to which the manufacturing of components and machinery shifts to China mainly through FDI, as is foreshadowed by the intentions of companies operating in China (Eberhardt and others 2004; Lall and Albaladejo 2004).[75]

How should China cement the country's trade relations with other countries? Given the surge in China's exports, there is a risk of trade disputes with other countries ("Trade Surpluses" 2005). China has already been involved in a number of antidumping claims. In total, 15 percent of the antidumping cases during 1995–2001 were against China;[76] in contrast, China initiated only 24 antidumping cases from 1997 to September 2003 and has never initiated a WTO trade panel (Mallon and Whalley 2004).[77] So far, most of the disputes have been resolved through bilateral means (Mallon and Whalley 2004). As the country's trade profile grows, China will need to work more actively with other countries to sustain

Table 3.15. Geographic Origin of China's Imports, Various Years
percent

Origin	1995	2000	2003	2004
Asia	47.1	50.6	66.1	65.8
ASEAN	7.4	9.8	11.5	11.2
Japan	21.9	18.4	18.0	16.8
Korea, Rep. of	7.8	10.3	10.4	11.1
Taiwan, China	11.2	11.3	12.0	11.5
European Union	17.0	13.7	13.2	12.5
United States	12.1	9.9	8.2	8.0

Source: For 1995 and 2000, Rumbaugh and Blancher 2003; for 2003 and 2004, National Bureau of Statistics of China, *China Statistical Yearbook,* 2005.

---

73. Latin America may see an increase in its exports of agricultural products to China (Shafaeddin 2002).
74. More than half of the overall export growth in Korea and Taiwan (China) comes from growth in exports to China (World Bank 2004d).
75. Multinational companies tend to source locally if local components can be sourced cheaper and quality can be assured. Sourcing locally will also assist in implementing just-in-time inventory systems (Eberhardt and others 2004).
76. Although in the past 10 years, China won 37 percent of these cases (Mallon and Whalley 2004).
77. Of these, 17 antidumping cases against other countries were initiated between July 2002 and June 2003 (Mallon and Whalley 2004).

harmonious trading relationships. One avenue is through regional trade agreements, especially where such measures can be stepping stones to global integration (Krumm and Kharas 2004; Sakakibara and Yamakawa 2004) and better regional coordination on other policy issues such as monetary, health, and competition policy.[78] Results of simulations point to overall welfare gains for the participating economies, so long as the trading bloc includes China, Japan, and Korea and entails minimal welfare losses for outsiders, so that the region retains its openness to the global market (Gilbert, Scollay, and Bora 2004).[79]

---

78. Much of the effort to achieve regional integration stems from the Asian financial crisis and frustration with the slow pace of multilateral agreements (Pangestu and Gooptu 2004). Given the small number of economies involved in the negotiations, bilateral and regional agreements are easier to negotiate. See Eichengreen (2004) on financial integration and Lloyd, Vautier, and Crampton (2004) on the benefits of harmonizing competition policy in East Asia. The threat of an avian flu pandemic spreading from Southeast Asia has increased the desirability of close cooperation on health issues.

79. Of course, the larger the number of economies included in the regional agreements, the greater the welfare gains and the smaller the impact on excluded economies. For details on the effects of various regional agreements in East Asia, see Gilbert, Scollay, and Bora (2004).

CHAPTER 4

Reducing Poverty and Achieving Interregional Balance

Growth of GDP and the shift of labor from agriculture to urban-industrial occupations (accompanied by remittances to rural households) are the strongest forces acting to reduce poverty, as they have been for the past two decades. Intersectoral transfer of workers also reduces income disparities. In other words, growth and migration out of the rural sector are likely to remain the principal means for achieving a *xiaokang* society. It is frequently maintained that their effects can be reinforced by more targeted interventions that selectively raise the incomes of rural households in the lower deciles and improve their access to social services, which lags that of households in urban areas.[1] The types of interventions that have received the most attention are efforts to increase the provision of education, health, social security, and infrastructure services to poorer

---

1. This depends on how well the intervention is targeted. Even though the official (Chinese) poverty headcount decreased from 125 million in 1985 to 50 million in 1997, the number of the rural population living in poor counties (with the expansion of the targeted areas) increased from 106 million to 199 million (Park, Wang, and Wu 2002). Furthermore, political considerations as well as economic ones influenced the designation as a poor county introduced in 1986. Once a county is designated as poor, delisting it becomes difficult, even when the income level rises above the poverty line. As a result, 20 percent of counties are designated as poor, although their income level is much higher than the official poverty line (Park, Wang, and Wu 2002).

households. The belief in the efficacy of such interventions stems directly from the proposition that human capital makes people more mobile,
improves job prospects, and raises earnings.[2] Improving the rural transport
infrastructure widens the economic options of rural households, encour-
ages production for the market, cuts down on marketing costs, and
induces diversification of the product mix toward cash crops as well as
diversification of labor into nonfarm activities.[3] A stronger safety net is a
means of preventing vulnerable people from descending into poverty and,
over the longer term, can bolster consumption propensities. This simple
and appealing logic underlies the poverty-alleviating programs implemented since the 1980s, including, for instance, the 8-7 National Poverty
Reduction Program initiated in 1994.[4]

The supply and quality of services, especially privately provided services, is still uneven across provinces, and this tends to be mirrored in the indicators of poverty. In poorer counties, households (especially of minorities)
typically have less access to services from public and private sources
("China's Rural Healthcare Crisis" 1999; Gao and others 2001; Low 2004;
Meng, Liu, and Shi 2000), and significant gender differences remain in
poor areas with respect to health and education (Taylor 2004a; World Bank
2004a).

While detailed data at the microlevel are not readily available, the
aggregate figures provide a sense of the prevailing fiscal disparities
among regions. Urban areas account for only 41 percent of the population, but they receive 60 percent of total government expenditure

---

2. See, for instance, Zhang, Huang, and Rozelle (2002). See also the survey of the literature
by Temple (1999).
3. Fan and Zhang (2004) find that infrastructure (measured by the number of telephones)
is positively correlated with the increase in production for both farm and nonfarm products, although the effects of infrastructure on nonfarm activities are much greater. Huang,
Rozelle, and Chang (2003) find that farmers farther from the market receive lower
prices.
4. The 8-7 program was introduced to lift the majority of the 80 million poor above the
official poverty line by 2000. Its aim was to (1) assist poor households with land improvements, shift toward higher-valued farm products, and improve access to off-farm employment opportunities; (2) provide all townships with roads, electricity, and water; (3) provide universal primary education and preventive and curative basic health care; (4) delist
successful counties from the list of counties designated as poor; (5) better manage the
funding earmarked to poverty alleviation; and (6) mobilize support from all government
ministries, agencies, and international organizations toward these goals, while maintaining
the subsidized loan program, food-for-work program, and government budgetary grants,
which were first introduced in 1986 (Wang, Li, and Ren 2003). See Park, Wang, and Wu
(2002) for the evaluation of antipoverty programs since 1986.

(Saich 2004). Own revenues per capita of the richest province, judged by revenue, are fifteen times those of the poorest region, while sub-provincial disparities among counties are significantly larger (Hofman and Guerra 2004). This fiscal disparity also translates into disparities in the indicators of service delivery. For instance, the number of hospital beds per 1,000 persons in rural areas declined from 1.5 in 1980 to 1.11 in 1998, while that in urban areas increased from 4.6 to 6.1 in the same period. Similarly, while rural areas saw a reduction in health care personnel, urban areas saw an increase (Kanbur and Zhang 2003; see table 4.1). Furthermore, four-fifths of rural households are without any insurance (although there is now a bare-bones government-subsidized community health care system for many counties) and need to pay "out of pocket" for medical services, leading to a reduction in visits to a doctor (Dong 2003).[5] The average rural health care cost has increased 75 percent since 1998 to Y97.7 (Taylor 2004a). A national survey in 2003 revealed that 25 percent of those who had some symptoms did not seek medical help, and 17.2 percent of persons who should have been hospitalized were not because of the cost of medical care (Saich 2004; see table 4.2). In Beijing, 30 percent of patients refused hospitalization, with 70 percent citing cost as the main reason for refusal. The government responded by cutting the retail price of 22 types of medicines

Table 4.1. Availability of Health Care Services in China, 1980–8
per 1,000 persons

Year	Hospital beds		Health care personnel persons	
	Urban	*Rural*	*Urban*	*Rural*
1980	4.57	1.48	7.82	1.81
1985	4.48	1.50	7.81	2.06
1990	5.81	1.37	9.15	1.89
1995	6.09	1.19	9.31	1.73
1998	6.08	1.11	9.16	1.71

Source: Kanbur and Zhang 2003.

---

5. The government's share of health expenditure is 37 percent of total health expenditure. Total health expenditure has increased from 3.8 percent of GDP in 1984 to 5.8 percent in 2002, mainly through an increase in private spending on health rather than an increase in government outlay (Saich 2004; Zhao 2005). Government expenditures account for 2 percent of GDP (World Bank 2003c). Public expenditure on education was 3 percent of GDP in 2001, although the 1985 Education Law called for increasing the spending to 4 percent of GDP (World Bank 2003c).

Table 4.2. Health Indicators in China, 1991–2000

Year	Infant mortality		Under-five mortality		Maternal mortality	
	Rural	Urban	Rural	Urban	Rural	Urban
1991	58	17	71	21	100	46
1992	53	18	66	21	98	43
1993	50	16	61	18	85	39
1994	46	16	57	18	78	44
1995	42	14	51	16	76	39
1997	38	13	49	16	80	38
1998	38	14	48	16	74	29
1999	38	12	48	14	80	26
2000	37	12	46	14	70	29

Source: Ministry of Public Health (2001).
Note: Infant mortality and under-five mortality rates are deaths per 1,000 live births. Maternal mortality rate is deaths per 10,000 live births.

4 percent starting in October 2005 ("Gouged" 2005). In the poorest counties and villages, the effects of morbidity on household welfare are likely to be substantial.

Similar disparities are prevalent in the sphere of education. In China's poorer provinces in 2001, only 70 percent of all students ultimately completed the nine years of compulsory schooling (see figure 4.1). The disparities for secondary and higher secondary schooling are even wider. For junior secondary schooling, enrollment in lagging provinces such as Gansu, Guizhou, and Qinghai averaged between 60 and 70 percent, compared with 99 percent in Zhejiang. For higher secondary education, the rates for the poorer inland provinces ranged between 30 and 40 percent, and dropout rates were also greater (World Bank 2003d). Rural children, especially girls, are more disadvantaged: they have lower enrollment and completion rates because, when faced with financial hardship, parents are more likely to withdraw daughters from school than sons (Connelly and Zheng 2003; Taylor 2004a).[6] This is reflected in fewer years of schooling for women across all provinces.

Government spending per student for education in provinces such as Gansu and Guizhou is well below that in the coastal provinces; typically, it is less than half. Hence households in these provinces pay higher fees

---

6. On the rural-urban education differentials, Taylor (2004a) and Wang (2004) note that the provincial Gini coefficient for education improved between 1990 and 2000, although regional disparities remain wide.

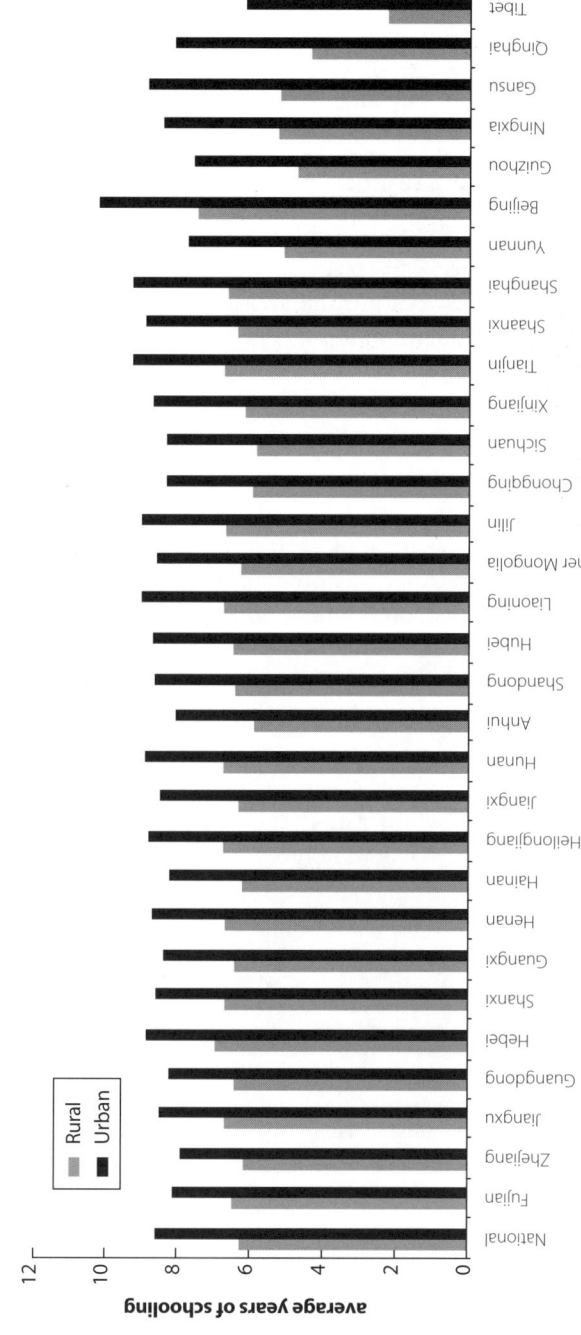

Figure 4.1. Average Years of Schooling in China's Provinces, by Rural or Urban Location, 2000

Source: Wang 2002.

and spend more on textbooks, supplies, and transportation (World Bank 2003d). These can amount to a sizable portion of the disposable income of rural households in the poorest counties, for instance, in Yunnan (Taylor 2004a).

Human Development Outcomes

Despite trends in the availability of publicly provided services, social indicators have improved steadily. Even as public health care has declined and the costs of health care services in rural areas have increased, health outcomes for the average rural inhabitant have risen year after year across all provinces. Infant mortality, under-five mortality, maternal mortality, and life expectancy have all improved in China's rural areas (table 4.2). These figures might mask underlying morbidity, but they do suggest that lower public spending and the fiscal constraints in poorer counties are not adversely affecting health outcomes.[7]

Statistics on education also point to improving education outcomes. For example, the average years of schooling are only slightly lower in the western region than in the coastal and central regions. Even in the poorer western region, the rate of enrollment in primary school is 95 percent for girls, compared with the national average of 99.1 percent, although the average years of schooling are shorter for girls, 4.8 years, than for boys, 6.7 years (Taylor 2004a). Moreover, even though the education resources per capita are much higher in the eastern region, each province in the central and western regions has raised the average number of years of schooling since 1982 by approximately the same amount (Tibet is the only outlier; see figure 4.2). This pattern persists through 2000, which is the last year for which data are available. The seemingly uniform improvement in average school years has occurred in spite of a decentralized and changing fiscal environment and the persistence of large fiscal disparities.[8] The data in figures 4.3 and 4.4 show that the poorer

---

7. Banister and Hill (2004) maintain that improvements in income and the quantity and quality of food as well as the provision of education, vaccination programs, and water supplies were the main factors responsible for the reduction in child mortality. Rising incomes and effective control of infectious disease led to the improvement in life expectancy across the entire age distribution (Banister and Hill 2004; Liu, Hsiao, and Eggleston 1999). On the issue of fiscal resources and interprovincial fiscal transfers, see World Bank (2002b, 2003c) and Dabla-Norris (2004).

8. In the mid-1990s, the central government's share in expenditure of 27 percent was extremely low compared with 54 percent in the United States, 66 percent in Brazil, and 60 percent in the Philippines (Dabla-Norris 2004). The center now finances close to half

Figure 4.2. Average Years of Schooling in China, by Region, 1982, 1990, and 2000

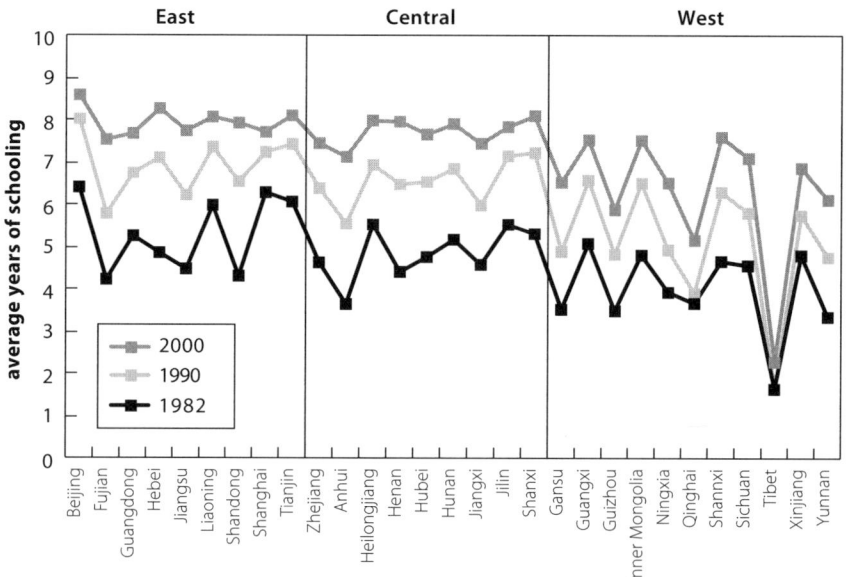

Source: Fan, Zhang, and Shang 2002.

provinces have, on average, been able to keep up with the changes in richer provinces with respect to other indicators, but the gaps have not narrowed. This phenomenon can be observed in other parts of the world as well, and, in general, there seems to be only a weak correlation between variation in spending levels and variation in outcomes. There is some indication for China, though, that persistent fiscal disparities lead to persistent differences in outcomes (Hofman and Guerra 2004). Moreover, aggregates could conceal variation in access across income strata. Finally, fiscal disparities are only part of the picture, as private contributions finance an increasing share of public services. While this may have been a viable model at the time because income disparities were low, the widening income disparities in China increase the risk that people from lower income strata will be excluded from using public services.

When we juxtapose health and education indicators with poverty headcounts and rural Gini coefficients, we find that poverty reduction slowed after the mid-1980s and continued declining modestly in the

_____

of local expenditures, through transfers, much of which are negotiated and ad hoc in nature (Dabla-Norris 2004). For details on the current intergovernmental fiscal relations, see World Bank (2002b).

Figure 4.3. Literacy Rate in China, by Region, 1982, 1990, and 2000

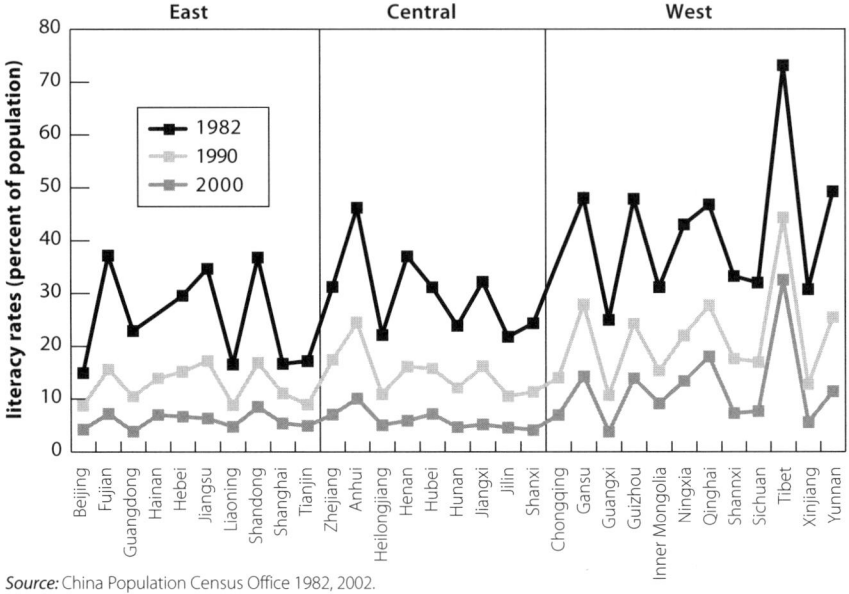

Source: China Population Census Office 1982, 2002.

Figure 4.4. Life Expectancy in China, by Region, 1990 and 2000

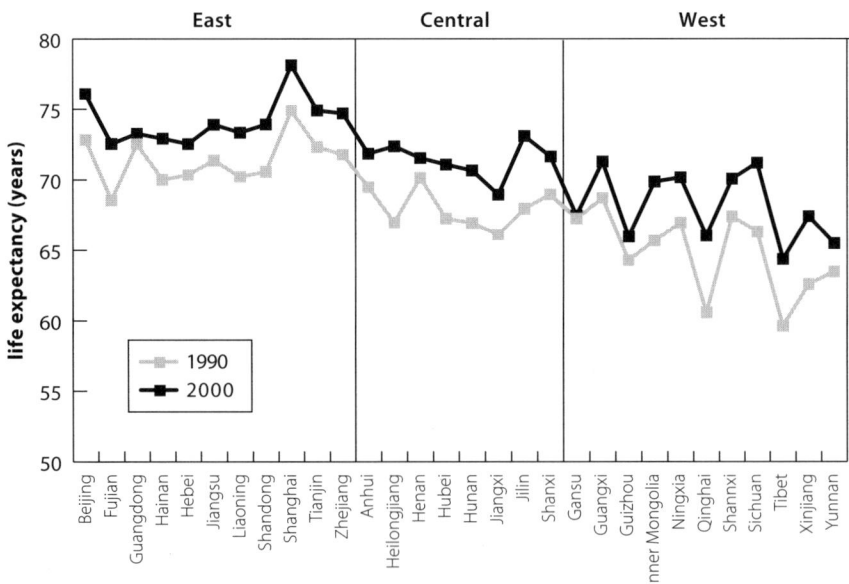

Source: China Population Census Office 1982, 2002.

1990s. Furthermore, rural inequality worsened in the 1990s, suggesting that better social indicators and antipoverty programs (for example, the 8-7 program) did not offset other factors influencing income disparities and the pace at which poverty is being reduced. Neither did the rising ratio of roads to provincial areas (see figure 4.5) or improved sanitation (see table 4.3).[9] In fact, Park, Wang, and Wu (2002) suggest that the returns to antipoverty programs were low. They find that income grew 2.28 percent faster in poor counties than in nonpoor ones during 1985–92, but only 0.91 percent faster during 1992 and 1995. The rate of return was estimated to be 12 and 16 percent, respectively, but it was less than half of these numbers once the administrative costs were factored in (Park, Wang, and Wu 2002).

Avenues to Balanced Development

In light of these trends, a strategy seeking to reduce poverty and inequality through higher outlay on social services and infrastructure would need to address three sets of questions. What composition of spending on services and modes of targeting these services will yield the highest measurable outcomes with respect to reduction in poverty and income equality? Because the quality and effective delivery of services is as crucial for outcomes as the volume of services, what are the relevant criteria for determining these two attributes of services, and how can these be enforced? What ought to be the basis for allocating responsibilities for these services and their financing among different levels of government, and how large should the role of private providers be?[10] In other words, what share of finances ought to be raised locally from user fees and local levies, and what share ought to be transferred from provincial and national governments?

---

9. The relationship that emerges from the Chinese experience is at odds with the findings of a cross-country study of the relationship between infrastructure and income inequality. This reveals a significant negative relationship between the stock of infrastructure and the Gini coefficient. Higher-quality infrastructure is also associated with greater income equality (Calderón and Chong 2004).

10. The health care services in China are delivered through a three-tier system: county general hospitals and clinics, township hospitals and clinics, and village clinics, which are operated by village health workers (Lim and others 2004). Financing for health services is determined at the county level, although 60 percent of outpatient services are provided by village clinics or private providers, while 25 percent (14 percent) are provided by township (county) hospitals. In order to pool the risk of insurance, the lowest appropriate level for financing health services should be the county, although education can be financed and provided at the village level (Saich 2004).

Figure 4.5. Road Length per Square Kilometer in China, by Region, 1990–2004

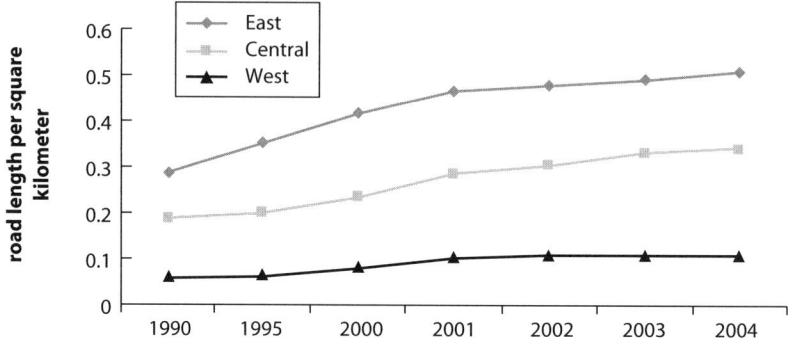

Source: National Bureau of Statistics of China, China Statistical Yearbook, various years; www.usacn.com (for provincial areas).

Table 4.3. Access to Sanitation in China, 1990 and 2000
percent of population with access

Indicator	1990	2000
Total	29	40
Rural	18	27
Urban	57	69

Source: World Bank 2004e.

The current state of our knowledge is such that there are no specific answers to these questions, although in some cases, plausible observations can be made, based on economic principles and on Chinese as well as cross-country experience.

On the question regarding the composition of spending and the gains from targeting, it is fair to say that usable knowledge to guide policy actions in China is quite sparse. Returns to education are in the range of 7 to 11 percent, with returns on postprimary education being greater than returns on primary education.[11] Hence, in principle, a desirable policy would be to promote increased public spending on school facilities and enrollment, supported by intergovernmental fiscal transfers that adequately meet expenditure assignments at the county level. But

---

11. Giles and others (2003) estimate returns of 7.5 to 9.1 percent. De Brauw and Rozelle (2002) estimate returns of 6.4 to 11 percent, with migrants showing higher returns. Heckman (2003) maintains that returns can go as high as 20–30 percent.

enrollment and school buildings do not generally lead to the outcomes being sought. Instead, the quality and content of the teaching, the skills of teachers, their motivation and presence in the schools, and the access of students to teaching materials are what produce results (Pritchett 2004). The problems at the county level in China have less to do with the adequacy of public funding than with how public resources are spent on schooling.[12] Often too much is expended on teaching staff so as to generate employment, and little effort is put into establishing and fulfilling the quality criteria that matter. Undoubtedly, while some of the poorer counties would benefit from additional funding, the broader gains that impinge on poverty and inequality will come from improvements in the quality of instruction and the content of education, which also would reduce the dropout rate.[13] The Ministry of Education could induce better outcomes by tracking completion rates in primary and secondary schools and publishing them nationally (Taylor 2004a). Such improvements would also affect the earnings prospects of those who migrate. Currently, the education provided is of little use to migrants for entry-level jobs in urban areas—construction work, unskilled factory labor, and housework. Vocational training now being offered in some counties through the Sunshine Program would be more helpful, as would be some modifications to the general school curriculum.[14] Increasing expenditures so as to raise the education levels of the rural populace will not encourage migration so long as migrants are forced to accept menial jobs in cities. In fact, the better educated might be less likely to move to cities (DFID 2004).

As with education, returns to better health are also large, and this would argue for more public funding in the poorer counties on public health services and preventive medicine.[15] Instead, central government spending on health care dropped from 2.0 percent of GDP in 1991 to 1.5 percent of GDP in 2000. But the deficiencies in health care may be related to the nature of the services themselves rather than the adequacy of public

---

12. For instance, inspections of 50 counties and county-level cities revealed that 43 cities misappropriated or defaulted on funds designated for schools, amounting to Y445 million ("Official Misusing Education" 2004).
13. Improving the quality of instruction entails, in part, ensuring that teachers diligently perform their assigned duties.
14. This program hopes to assist some 35 million farmers during this decade.
15. Almost 90 percent of deaths are now the result of noncommunicable diseases and injuries especially traffic- and workplace-related injuries (Claeson, Wang, and Hu 2004).

resources. The services rendered by public facilities are of low quality, which forces people to seek unregulated private providers who also supply mediocre services, as in other lower- and lower-middle-income counties.[16] In public facilities, low morale and absenteeism, high prices, substandard quality, low use of equipment, and inappropriate and excessive prescription of medications and other interventions to generate additional income for the service provider combine to diminish the efficiency of public health inputs.[17] The problems are aggravated in the Chinese context by the absence of uniform norms for quantity and quality as well as by weak enforcement of existing norms and licensing requirements.[18]

Most observers start by noting the disparity in education, health, and transport indicators across provinces and counties and from there conclude that the levels in the poorer areas ought to be raised. The simple rule of thumb is to provide more, especially when public spending on education and health is lower in China than in many East Asian and industrial coun-

---

16. A study by Banerjee, Deaton, and Duflo (2004, p. 330) on rural Rajasthan in India also shows that public health care is "abysmal." Regardless of where they operate (in rural-urban or public-private), most doctors are not satisfied with their income, level of skills, opportunities for upgrading their skills, interactions with other doctors, and the availability of supporting hardware and services (for example, X-rays). Almost all doctors agree that the private sector should be regulated to ensure the quality and safety of patients if it is to play a major role in China. This is based on the general perception that the medical licenses are "for sale" with minimal supervision and that there is widespread sale of fake drugs and overprescription for profit (Lim and others 2004). Despite these concerns, private doctors flourish in China, as in other countries, because they charge lower fees than public hospitals, offer flexible operating hours and payment methods, attend to their patients more promptly, and are more responsive to patients' needs (Lewis, Eskeland, and Traa-Valerezo 2004; Lim and others 2004).

17. Many public health institutions suffer from low use (Smith, Wong, and Zhao 2004). For instance, even though the revenues generated from high-technology diagnostic tools and services such as computed tomography and magnetic resonance imaging scans are an important source of finance for many health care providers, studies find that these services are mostly underused by between 25 and 33 percent (Liu, Nolan, and Wen 2004). In rural clinics, studies find that more than 98 percent of the drugs dispensed are unnecessary, leading to higher costs of medical help in rural areas (Meng, Li, and Eggleston 2004, "China's Challenges" 2006).

18. For instance, absenteeism of health care workers is a major problem in India. Since most facilities are manned by only one nurse, absenteeism leads to closure of the health facility. In fact, facilities are closed 56 percent of the regular hours of operation. To make matters worse, the times when the clinics are closed is fairly random, leaving patients guessing (Banerjee, Deaton, and Duflo 2004). Despite this, poor households spend more than 7 percent of their monthly expenditure on health care (Banerjee, Deaton, and Duflo 2004). In the case of China, all doctors are registered and licensed, although there is no specialty certification following passage of the Act of Medical Practitioner (Lim and others 2004).

tries (see table 4.4). But basic indicators of education, health, and transport have been rising steadily in even the least-developed provinces in the face of an apparent deterioration in publicly supplied social services. The big gains in health, for example, have accrued from better sanitation, clean water, improved nutrition, and past campaigns to control infectious diseases. These laudable campaigns have run out of steam, although the significance of preventive medicine and an efficient public health surveillance system is greater than ever. Parents have to pay for childhood immunization, which is reducing the number of children who are immunized against common infectious diseases such as measles and whooping cough. The inadequacy of the system for treating, tracking, and counseling people who have contracted tuberculosis is resulting in the rise of multidrug-resistant strains and to the spread of the disease. Changing food habits—in particular, the greatly increased consumption of meat and fats—are increasing the incidence of obesity, which, if not checked through public health measures, will lead to a surge in diseases such as diabetes and hypertension (Du and others 2004; Watts 2005). Furthermore, the experience with the SARS outbreak and the threats posed by diseases such as avian flu underscore the need for strengthening key parts of the public health infrastructure ("China: Towards 'Xiaokang'" 2004). There is scope for an increase in the level of public funding for preventive medicine countrywide, but, in poorer counties overall, a program to expand outlay on health should be predicated on a careful assessment of which expenditures promise the highest returns. Raising the efficiency of existing expenditures and physical facilities through better regulation, monitoring, and competition from private providers may yield higher dividends. However, profit motive is a double-edged sword, encouraging the overprescription of newer and expensive drugs and excessive use of diagnostic technologies, the costs of which are borne largely by patients (Wang

Table 4.4. Education Expenditure as a Share of GDP in Select Countries, 2000

Country	Percent of GDP
China	2.9
Japan	3.6
Korea, Rep. of	4.4
Germany	4.5
United Kingdom	4.6
United States	5.2

Source: OECD 2000; For China, National Bureau of Statistics of China, *China Statistical Yearbook,* 2001.

2005). Health care insurance, apart from safeguarding more equitable access to services, could play a significant role in enforcing cost-efficiency of service providers by establishing eligibility rules for funding. Whereas in the late 1970s, health insurance was available to more than 85 percent of all Chinese, currently only about 20 percent of rural residents and 55 percent of urban residents have health insurance. Moreover, even the insured have had to pay much higher co-payments and fees for services as costs have risen. This is also the case for the government-subsidized, community-based insurance schemes introduced in recent years and being expanded in urban areas (Akin, Dow, and Lance 2004; UNDP 2005; Wang 2005, "China's Challenges" 2006).[19] In some countries, league tables among hospitals are used to provide consumers with better-informed choices among facilities. These then are some of the measures to be considered in crafting a health strategy for a *xiaokang* society.

In the education sector, the governance of schools could be boosted by innovations such as school boards, parent-teacher associations, and capitation grants that provide parents with a choice among schools and exert competitive pressures on individual schools to deliver better services. Independent school inspections that enforce quality standards tied to eligibility for public funding could further improve quality.

Some research on other developing countries using finely disaggregated poverty map data suggests that microlevel targeting could be effective in delivering services to the poor (Elbers and others 2004). The Bank's own project-related activities in Yunnan are oriented toward the poorest villages and specifically designed to provide services for the disadvantaged, especially women. The very limited experience with such interventions does not yet tell us whether more spending on health and less on transport or whether a particular mode of targeting will yield specific outcomes, not the least because local governments will often divert revenues to other uses or spend too large a share on hiring staff. It is also uncertain whether such intervention can bring about longer-lasting changes.[20]

The roles of different levels of government and of private providers are also not firmly anchored to an analytic and empirical base. The fact is that the responsibility for providing services devolved onto township,

---

19. The publicly provided basic health care system introduced in 2002 covered over a billion people by 2004, and in 2005 the subsidy was raised from Y10 per year to Y20 (UNDP 2005).
20. Schultz (2004) is doubtful that the evidence supports the efficacy of targeting measures used worldwide.

county, and prefectural governments many decades ago, with fiscal responsibilities being formalized in the mid-1980s (Lin and Liu 2000).[21] The township-level governments often are not assigned the formal tax revenues to fulfill their expenditure assignments. Increasingly, therefore, public services are financed through off-budget sources and through out-of-pocket expenditures by households. For instance, the out-of-pocket expenditure for health care, noted earlier, increased from 16 percent in 1980 to 50–75 percent in 2001–3; for education, it increased from 2.3 to 12.5 percent between 1990 and 1998 (Kanbur and Zhang 2003; Wang 2005).[22] This may suggest that a lack of fiscal resources (from assigned taxes and transfers) reduced the access to publicly supplied services, especially to the rural poor. It also assumes that the fiscal resources are efficiently used, when typically they are not. In some cases, local governments would have sufficient means from tax revenues, extra-budgetary revenues, and off-budget revenues if they would use the resources more efficiently.[23] Hence one approach that has been proposed is to address problems such as weak administrative capability and insufficient accountability, even when these are supplemented by earmarked transfers from higher-level governments.[24] The fee-for-tax reform implemented in 2003 and the reassignment of expenditures for teachers to the county level are a case in point.

A second approach that has been proposed is to reassign some of the services from lower levels to county governments and also to reform the tax-and-transfer system to adequately support the provision of services so that county governments can dispense with off-budget fees to meet their

---

21. On the structure of local government, see Zhang (2003).
22. Using household survey data from 1988 and 1995, Gustafsson and Li (2004) show that household expenditure increased as much as 192 percent for health care and 165 percent for education during this period. The share of expenditure on education increased from 1 to 2.2 percent of total household expenditures, while for health care, it increased from 1.6 to 3.6 percent. The expenditure share by deciles decreased rapidly.
23. Efforts to downsize governments so as to reduce expenditures on staff costs have not proven effective in part because decentralization reduces the leverage of the central government (Burns 2003).
24. Case studies of rural Ninglang County in Shaanxi Province reveal that most of the budget allocated for health is consumed by personnel costs, and the subsidies program does not promote efficiency or better quality. When earmarked transfers for education are received, they are often used to raise the salaries of teachers and to hire additional teachers, even though these schools already have enough teachers based on the state guidelines (Weist 2004). Similarly, staffing levels for health facilities can be excessive. One example from Hunan reveals that staffing costs are more than twice as much as the budget allocated for health (Saich 2004).

expenditure requirements (Saich 2004).[25] Social protection programs such as pension and unemployment benefits are best administered at the national level, which allows risks to be pooled over a larger number of people (Dabla-Norris 2004). A third approach, which is to depend more on private providers, has already been adopted de facto and may account for the favorable movement in social indicators.[26] How much more of a shift in this direction is desirable—with a commensurate reduction in taxes and fees—remains an open question.

While there is no shortage of proposals for reforming social policies, administrative mechanisms, taxes, and intergovernmental fiscal transfers, the case for these is not always based on a diagnosis of the problem and analysis that traces the likely consequences of policy actions.[27] Too often, policy recommendations on administrative and fiscal reforms either are of a general nature and based on broad qualitative assessments or are grounded in a few case studies whose general applicability is not well established. Inevitably, these do not achieve planned objectives or achieve the objectives only partially. A more analytical and empirical approach, which complements any additional fiscal transfers with the beefing up of governance mechanisms for those funds (at the local government level as well as at the level of public service units), would be a better bet. This becomes all the more urgent now that the government has decided to allocate part of the enterprise income tax for equalization purposes.

Inequality and Development

Research to date has helped to identify the characteristics of the rural poor and their geographic distribution. Frequently, they live in remote areas, belong to ethnic minorities (25 percent), have large families with fewer working members, farm poorer-quality land with limited access to water, are illiterate, and have lesser access to public health services, technical sup-

---

25. Decentralization of public services has been pursued vigorously since the 1990s, with the aim to improve the access to as well as the quality of services in local areas. However, the evidence so far has been mixed. In some counties, decentralization has led to corruption when accountability is absent and to a deterioration in access and the quality of services when local administrative capacity is lacking (Khaleghian 2004).

26. A three-pillar pension scheme would combine employer contributions, a fully funded individual account, and a supplementary optional pension.

27. See Ahmad, Singh, and Lockwood (2004) for analysis of the changing value added tax system in China and its implication for the fiscal transfer between the center and the provinces. Introducing a rule-based transparent transfer system would be one course of policy action (Dabla-Norris 2004).

port, markets, and credit (Taylor 2004a; UNDP 2005). The majority of the poor are in some of the central provinces, such as Ningxia and Shanxi, or in western and southwestern provinces, such as Guizhou and Yunnan, with the poorest counties being where the land is hilly, degraded, and dry.

Research also suggests that the Gini coefficient in China is rising, even though the average rural-urban income disparity remains largely unchanged. The main factors at work are the shifts in substantial numbers of workers to better-paid rural, off-farm, and urban employment, while significant numbers of the poorest households remain trapped in poverty, linked to location, ethnicity, illiteracy, and gender. Many of these do not receive remittances from urban areas because family members do not participate in urban migration.

For the majority of the poor, migration and income growth may provide the stepping stones out of poverty without the need for large increases in social spending. But for the poor in the more remote areas, climbing out of poverty may require more inclusive and possibly targeted social and safety net programs (such as the rural *dibao*) backed by larger fiscal transfers that are allocated more efficiently.[28] The Eleventh Plan offers an opportunity to introduce such programs and push China closer to a *xiaokang* society. But simply calling for more spending is unlikely to deliver results.[29] The health policy objective needs to be targeted explicitly toward the poor rather than be stated in terms of population averages. Otherwise, the additional resources will tend to subsidize the rich rather than the poor. Expanding the voluntary Medical Finance Assistance Scheme for the poor offers one policy handle (Gwatkin, Bhuiya, and Victora 2004). At the implementation stage, the government has many different means to achieve better results by undertaking better targeting, providing cash payments for using services (rather than subsidizing the supply of services), and partnering with nongovernmental organizations and local communities (Gwatkin, Bhuiya, and Victora 2004; Taylor 2004a). Obtaining results with geographic targeting requires paying close attention to many details of methodology, local institutions, design, implementation, monitoring, corrective actions, and regular assessment of outcomes. Very little of this spade work has been done; as a result, there

---

28. In Yunnan's Xinghang County in 2003, health centers received 28 percent of the county budget. However, just 1.7 percent of the funds eventually reached the village health centers (Taylor 2004a).

29. In fact, the Ministry of Finance raised transfers to county governments to offset the losses from inadequate fee revenues. The amount was Y30.5 billion in 2003.

are few tried and tested policies to put into practice. The authorities would be better advised to collect detailed data and conduct well-designed experiments to identify and elaborate policies that would lead to desired and measurable results in China's poorest provinces.

Alleviating poverty and diminishing inequality require much more than spending more money on public services. The priority should be to seek policies that will produce results under specific socioeconomic circumstances. These policies are likely to involve managerial capacity building, a more participatory approach, public-private partnerships in the delivery of services, and a deeper understanding of how local and nationwide developments affect the dynamics of poverty in different parts of China (Taylor 2004a).

CHAPTER 5

Conserving Energy and Water Resources

A growing population, rising per capita incomes, and urbanization inevitably entail higher consumption of resources, particularly energy and water. It is no surprise, therefore, that China's use of resources has risen, but the scale of consumption and the speed with which it has increased and is increasing are matters of concern. Looking ahead, managing resource use will be a critical issue for policy makers, and energy consumption will have broader consequences for the global community as well.

Energy Intensity

The energy intensity of China's GDP has been declining steadily since the early 1980s as a result of changes in the composition of industry, improved technologies, and incentives that have encouraged greater energy efficiency.[1] In 2002 China needed less than half of the energy per unit of GDP used in 1993 (Smil 2002) and only one-quarter of that used in 1980 (Zhang 2003). The income elasticity of energy consumption was

---

1. Total energy use and, in some cases, the energy intensity of GDP have also fallen in other transition economies, although, in almost all cases, energy intensity was higher than that of the United States in 1999 (Cornillie and Fankhauser 2004).

0.34 for the period from 1991 to 1997, which is close to the income elasticity of high-income countries: low- and middle-income countries tend to have elasticities greater than 1 (Zhang 2003). Although this is an impressive achievement, China's energy intensity in 2005 remains high compared with that of European countries and Japan, and energy use in many applications is far less efficient than in more developed industrial economies. Energy consumption in most standard industrial processes still remains 20–100 percent higher in China than in developed countries. Residential buildings in China are estimated to consume 50–100 percent more energy for space heating than buildings in similar climatic zones in Western Europe or North America but provide far less comfort.

Three developments can reduce the energy intensity of an economy. First, as incomes rise, the mix of industry changes, with the share of industry and, in particular, services rising and that of agriculture declining. While industrialization leads to an increase in energy intensity, the move toward services has the opposite effect. Second, within each sector of the economy, firms can take measures to improve energy efficiency. Finally, a country can change the mix of energy sources, from coal to oil and natural gas, which are more efficient than coal.

The rapid reduction in China's energy intensity in the past 20 years was achieved mainly through improvements in energy efficiency (often through technological changes and the introduction of better equipment, such as the replacement of boilers) rather than through broad sectoral shifts, although structural change within industries and subindustries played a major role. A major impetus for this change was the price of energy: a study of 2,500 firms by Fisher-Vanden and others (2004) found that the price effect accounts for 55 percent of the reduction in energy use, while 17 percent is the result of R&D efforts and 12 percent is traceable to different types of ownership.[2] The remaining 20 percent is attributed to changes in the structure of industries.[3]

In the medium term, China is unlikely to realize a significant reduction in energy intensity by changing the energy mix, as other countries

---

2. They find that foreign-invested firms are the most efficient firms in terms of energy use, followed by firms with investment from Hong Kong (China), Macao, and Taiwan (China). As one would expect, state-owned enterprises are the least-efficient users of energy (Fisher-Vanden and others 2004).

3. Between 1990 and 1997, 88 percent of industry energy savings were due to real intensity change, and the rest were attributed to change in the structure of industries and a shift to less energy-intensive activities (Zhang 2003).

have done. This is primarily because China is the largest producer of coal, a fact that is reflected in the sources of energy used in 2002: 71 percent of energy from coal, 17 percent from petroleum, 9 percent from hydropower, 3 percent from natural gas, and less than 1 percent from nuclear power (Steinfeld 2004b, p. 8).[4] Although further investment in natural gas infrastructure and nuclear power plants is planned, these are not likely to account for much more than 6 and 4 percent of the energy produced by 2010 and 2025, respectively.[5] Primary energy demand in 2020 will vary between 2.5 billion and 3.2 billion tons of coal equivalent, depending primarily on whether effective energy conservation policies and measures can be implemented (World Bank 2004c). In view of the energy resources available in China, coal is expected to continue dominating the composition of energy. Demand for raw coal is expected to increase from the current 1.6 billion tons per year to more than 2.5 billion tons per year. Crude oil demand is expected to increase to more than 500 million tons, of which more than half is likely to be imported. Demand for electric power capacity is expected to reach more than 1,000 gigawatts, up from 381 gigawatts in 2004. Oil and gas-fired capacity will continue to play a marginal role. Even if the government realizes its ambitious targets of adding 40 gigawatts of nuclear capacity and developing 63 percent of China's 380 gigawatts of economically exploitable hydropower potential by 2020, a large part of the additional capacity will have to come from coal-fired power plants.

Reducing energy intensity will require a multifaceted approach because of (1) dependence on coal and (2) the transport of less energy-dense coal using the rail or road network (Steinfeld 2004b). Furthermore, as China urbanizes and the use of automobiles increases, restraining the growth of energy consumption will also require the coordinated use of policy instruments. But the likelihood is that China's dependence on external sources of petroleum products will rise, and, with this, the issue

---

4. In 1977 coal accounted for 80 percent, oil for 17 percent, hydropower for 2 percent, and natural gas for 1 percent ("Geologic of China's Oil" 1979).

5. Since the mid-1990s, natural gas has been receiving substantial attention and investment, and it is expected to account for 6 percent of consumption by 2010. Similarly, while China's installed capacity to generate nuclear power had increased from 2.1 to 5.4 gigawatts by 2003, nuclear power still accounted for less than 1 percent of energy production. With further investment, the capacity could account for 4 percent (by adding 19 gigawatts by 2025), but it would still be rather miniscule compared with other energy sources. Hence investment in nuclear power is unlikely to solve China's near-term energy problems (Steinfeld 2004b, p. 9).

of energy security will come to the forefront. As globalization proceeds, multinational companies will continue to locate manufacturing activities, which are more energy intensive than other activities, in China (Fisher-Vanden and others 2004; Steinfeld 2004b; Zhang 2003).

Energy Policy

In light of the above, energy policy during the next decade could proceed down two parallel tracks—one focusing on improving efficiency and the other focusing on energy security. Greater efficiency in energy use can be achieved by (1) liberalizing the energy market to reflect market conditions; (2) improving the regulation and enforcement of existing regulations and imposing higher energy-efficiency standards for buildings, appliances, and automobiles; and (3) improving the "quality" of coal by washing, for example. To achieve energy security, it is essential to diversify both the mix of primary energy and its sourcing from different countries.

The findings of Fisher-Vanden and others (2004) suggest that users do conserve energy if prices go up: more than 50 percent of the energy-efficiency gain is attributed to a change in prices. Currently, oil and electricity prices only partially reflect world market conditions, leading to rising demand. The domestic price set by the National Development and Reform Commission is a mix of world market prices, a domestic shadow price of production, and a markup for distribution.[6] The resulting gasoline prices are lower than in China's comparators. Even though the government raised the cap on retail gasoline prices to $0.41 per liter, this is well below the price in the world market, and the retail price of mid-octane gas is nearly $0.10 per liter less than the average price in the United States, the country with the lowest fuel prices in the industrial world. Under the circumstances, higher fuel taxes may be called for to reflect the long-term marginal costs of energy and the cost of environmental damage ("Step by Step" 2004). Electricity prices are, on average, covering the cost of generation, but these reflect the cost of subsidized credits and exclude the environmental damage imposed by power generation. Moreover, large-volume industrial users are cross-subsidizing urban households; as a result, pricing promotes the acquisition of household appliances and higher levels of use, exacerbating the shortages of gener-

---

6. Since the beginning of 2004, the price of gasoline has increased 29 percent ("China Continues " 2005).

ating capacity (Steinfeld 2004b).[7] Correct pricing of electricity is crucial if more efficient end use is to be achieved. Similarly, by changing the rate of the fuel tax, governments can influence private automobile use and stimulate the demand for more fuel-efficient vehicles.

Efficiency of energy production and distribution also needs to be addressed. For power, integration of the six regional grids and promotion of a competitive market for electricity are keys for achieving this. Through interconnection, energy-rich regions in the west will be able to deliver power to coastal areas with power shortages. The central China and northern China grids have already been connected, and most of the regional and provincial grids were interconnected by 2005. A national grid is planned for 2010. By 2020 around 80–100 gigawatt capacity of electricity could be transferred from the west of China to the east and south.

China must continue to foster competitive power markets, starting with generation in the short term and extending to the wholesale level in the medium term and the retail level over the long term. In the first stage, all generators sell their output to a mandatory energy pool operated by the regional or provincial single buyer. The first stage is a critical first step in that it builds the foundation and capacity for later stages. In this phase, a common market-clearing pool price will be determined by the price of the last generator dispatched to meet total demand of the system. In the second stage, competition at the wholesale level is introduced, allowing distributors and eligible industrial customers to participate in the market by contracting directly with generators and purchasing power from the mandatory pool. In the third stage, retail competition is introduced, enabling all consumers to participate in the market by choosing their electricity retailer. This last stage requires separating the operation and management of the distribution network from commodity trading. The phased approach allows a smooth transition by building the skills and institutional capacity needed to manage, operate, and regulate wholesale and retail competitive markets.

Access to the grid must be given to any firm, including new entrants, able to supply electricity. This will require greater capability for regulato-

---

7. This can be seen from the difference in income elasticity of 0.34 at the national level (Zhang 2003), compared with income elasticity of 0.7 for urban residents (Henderson 2004b). Also, in rural areas, the estimated energy-price elasticity for color television, washing machine, and refrigerator ownership is –0.91, –1.26, and –1.67, respectively. These elasticities are much larger than those for income elasticity—0.14, 0.21, and 0.29—suggesting that the price of electricity significantly influences the decision to purchase modern household appliances (Rong and Yao 2003).

ry oversight (Steinfeld 2004b). These changes are necessary, as increasing numbers of electricity users will not be industries with steady demand for electricity, but urban residents with more fluctuating demand. The liberalization of the energy market to better reflect market conditions would lead to greater efforts at conservation and, as an added advantage, allow more alternative energy producers to enter the market at peak times (Steinfeld 2004b).[8] As with any economic activity, the energy market should be integrated, at least regionally, to reap the full benefits from improvements in energy production and distribution.[9]

Liberalization in the oil and gas sector is far behind liberalization in the power sector. As a result, efficiency is lagging, and penetration of gas use is low. An important step in modernization of the oil and gas sector would be to develop an oil and gas regulatory system. The policy role of government must be separate from its regulatory responsibilities, and enterprises should not be involved in either. China has the opportunity to make a fresh start in this field and create a modern, efficient, and effective regulatory structure. This reform will require the creation of a level regulatory playing field, administered by an independent commission or commissions that will take over environmental, technical, operational, economic, regulatory, and licensing functions from a number of existing agencies.

Apart from restructuring of the power industry, the imposition of tougher energy-efficiency standards is the most cost-effective way to achieve both supply constraints and energy security in China (Larson and others 2003). Unlike other countries, China's vast and rising appetite for energy will affect the world market. In 2004, as China's oil consumption rose to 6.68 million barrels per day, with imports accounting for 40 percent, 30 percent of global growth in oil consumption came from China ("China Continues" 2005; "What Goes Up" 2006; "Oily Diplomacy" 2006). Firms—foreign or domestic—supplying goods to China will have to innovate to meet domestic standards. Similarly, Chinese firms should develop energy-efficient products, which will be in demand elsewhere in the future. Thus, by imposing tougher standards, the government can cre-

---

8. The first step taken was to allocate transmission assets to the National Grid Corporation and the South China Grid Corporation and to create the State Electricity Regulatory Commission. However, the power to set prices still resides with the National Development and Reform Commission ("China: Capacity Expansion" 2004).

9. Simulation results show that, although efficiency can be improved by deregulating the energy market in Shandong (energy exporter) and in Shanghai (energy importer) independently, the greatest improvements can be achieved by integrating these two markets (Gnansounou and Dong 2004).

ate incentives for domestic firms to upgrade their capabilities and enhance their competitiveness (Steinfeld 2004b). One important area in this regard is the fuel efficiency of automobiles, which affects emissions.[10] The global trend is to further reduce the emissions from automobiles.[11] European automakers agreed to cut emissions 25 percent by 2008, and California is drafting a regulation requiring 30 percent less carbon dioxide by 2009 in addition to requiring 10 percent of cars sold in California to meet zero-emission standards. Such measures will be needed if China is to steadily raise efficiency and lower emissions. Moreover, if China is to leapfrog into new energy technologies such as fuel cells, which are currently much more expensive than even the hybrid vehicles, then a coordination of the efforts of the government and the auto companies will be required to conduct the research, trials and eventually the investment in infrastructure ("Clean Machine" 2004; "Driven by the Oil Price" 2004; Gallagher 2006, Ahman 2006, and Zhao and Melaina 2006).[12]

Second, because coal remains the primary source of energy, China needs to improve the efficiency of coal use and reduce emissions through coal cleaning, pulverization, liquefaction, and gasification (Steinfeld 2004b).[13] Locating generating plants near the mouth of mines and transmitting electricity via high-voltage lines would reduce pollution near urban areas and lessen the burden on railroads. By pulverizing coal, power plants could extract 40 percent of the energy contained in coal, compared with only 5 percent by simply burning raw coal ("Future Is Clean" 2004). In addition, liquefaction and gasification would facilitate the capture and sequestration

10. Carbon dioxide emissions per capita were 2.2 million metric tons in 2000, a slight increase from 2.1 million metric tons in 1990 (World Bank 2004e).
11. Currently the Chinese standards are equivalent to the European standards in 1994. Much of Beijing's pollution comes from automobiles. For instance, 92 percent of carbon monoxide, 94 percent of hydrocarbons, and 68 percent of sulfur oxide are traceable to auto emissions. The government is considering levying a tax based on engine size ("Dramatic Change" 2005). In order to reduce pollution from auto emissions, the quality of fuel also needs to be improved, since part of the reason for high emissions is the poor quality of fuel, which has a much higher content of sulfur than gasoline in developed countries (Gallagher 2006).
12. Toyota began producing its hybrid car in China in December 2005 through a joint venture with FAW.
13. Coal cleaning can reduce the discharge of particles and sulfur, contributing to the improvement in local environment. However, carbon dioxide discharge will increase because the efficiency gains in energy use will expand the economy (Glomsrod and Wei 2005). See Nolan, Shipman, and Rui (2004) for details on the coal liquefaction technology. During the winter months, 50 percent of rail capacity is used to transport coal (Woetzel 2003).

of carbon dioxide, reducing the emission of greenhouse gasses in addition to sulfur dioxide (Larson and others 2003; Steinfeld 2004b).

Renewable energy sources are likely to play a more important role in China, even though their contribution is likely to remain modest overall. The government is already committed to the Mid- and Long-Term Plan on Renewable Energy Development, which will significantly expand capacity in water, wind, and biomass energy. At the same time, more can be done. Adoption and implementation of the planned Renewable Energy Promotion Law is a step in the right direction, but this should be complemented by appropriate pricing of other energy sources, integration of the power grid, and peak-load pricing, which can improve the economic viability of existing renewable energy sources, as well as technological developments that could boost the efficiency of renewable energy sources.

More generally, to facilitate the move toward an energy-efficient and environmentally friendly economic system, China could boost its support for technological development in these fields. This would also contribute to the development of core technological competence of domestic firms (Steinfeld 2004b). Rather than pursuing targeted industrial policies, technology policies are more sensible, especially for clean-coal technology, as the use of coal worldwide is increasing; possibly also on fuel cell–related technologies, although the payoff from these is more uncertain ("Future Is Clean" 2004; Solomon and Banerjee 2006).[14]

From the perspective of energy security, China's concerns arise mainly from the heavy reliance on imported oil. The share of imported oil is expected to rise to well over 50 percent by 2010 (Steinfeld 2004b), of which two-thirds or more is likely to come from the Middle East ("China: Strategic Oil Reserve" 2003; Li 2003). One policy is to buffer against sudden short-term changes in global production levels. This could be achieved by building enough storage for reserves, as many oil-importing countries do today. China is exploring the possibility of increasing storage to the 90-day level suggested by the International Energy Agency ("China May Triple" 2004; "China: Strategic Oil Reserve" 2003).[15]

---

14. For instance, 33 percent of the electricity consumed in Britain comes from coal, 50 percent in Germany and the United States, and 75 percent in India ("Future Is Clean" 2004).

15. China expects to have 30 days of reserves in storage by 2010 at a cost of Y10 billion. This could be raised to 90 days by 2020 for an additional outlay of an estimated $11 billion. Japan holds reserves equivalent to 150 days of consumption ("China: Strategic Oil Reserve" 2003).

The other policy is to pursue energy diversification more actively, especially as the global production of oil is expected to decline in the future (Hallock and others 2004).[16] One option being explored in conjunction with Shell is to construct plants in Ningxia and Shaanxi to convert coal into petroleum, thereby using China's 130 billion tons of recoverable coal reserves more rapidly ("China Broadens" 2004). At present, the share of natural gas and nuclear power is relatively small, but it could rise in the future.[17] The demand for natural gas in 2010 is projected to be 100 billion cubic meters, with production capacity of 70 billion cubic meters; in 2020 demand and productive capacity could reach 140 billion–200 billion cubic meters and 100 billion cubic meters, respectively (Nolan, Shipman, and Rui 2004). Natural gas is receiving increasing attention because it is available domestically and is relatively clean. To increase the use of natural gas, China is investing in the vast infrastructure for piping the gas from producing areas, laying the local distribution network, and building the port facilities to import more natural gas, especially from Asia, where additional capacity of 120 billion cubic meters is available (Woetzel 2003).[18] A west-east pipeline brings gas from 14 fields in the Tarim Basin all the way across China to Baihe Town in Shanghai; the 4,200-kilometer pipeline, which has a capacity of 12 billion cubic meters, was constructed between July 2002 and September 2004 at a cost of approximately $17 billion ("West-East Gas" 2004a, 2004b). One advantage of natural gas over oil is that natural gas is distributed internationally more evenly than oil, although three-quarters of the known reserves are in the Middle East and Russia ("Future's a Gas" 2004).

The geographic location of energy sources could also be diversified. In 2003, 50 percent of China's crude oil was from the Middle East, 22 percent was from Asia, Africa, and 18 percent was from Africa ("Oil and Politics" 2004). More than 60 percent of the tankers pass through the

---

16. Global production will start to decline sometime between 2004 and 2037. In addition, the number of oil-exporting countries will decline from the current 35 to as few as 12 by 2030 (Hallock and others 2004).

17. The plan for the nuclear power expansion is ambitious, adding 27 gigawatts of capacity by 2020, possibly with the participation of foreign firms ("China Sees Role" 2004). The new, advanced light-water reactors, incorporating a passive emergency core and containment cooling system, are much simpler in design and less costly in addition to being safer and more reliable. Four such reactors are already operating in Japan, and many more are operating around the world. China is building two such reactors, with assistance from France (Taylor 2004b).

18. As much as half of the natural gas consumed is supplied by imports (Li 2003).

Strait of Malacca, a vulnerable and congested passageway (Nolan, Shipman, and Rui 2004). Thus the diversification of oil imports needs to focus on Central Asia Africa, and Russia, where competition from other countries is severe (such as competition with Japan for the pipeline from Russia).[19] However, so far China has made limited progress in securing oil fields in the former Soviet Union (Nolan, Shipman, and Rui 2004).[20]

The growing size of China's economy and the speed with which China is being drawn into the global system is introducing new complexities. International economic relations take on a far larger significance. China's growth strategy must increasingly factor in the implications for its trading partners and for key commodity markets. Because of its size, China is also in a stronger position to take more of a leadership role in defining trading arrangements that promote trade and minimize tensions.

Distribution of Water Resources

No other resource can substitute for water. As China and other countries are finding, a scarcity of water can be a binding constraint on agricultural production, industrial development, and the growth of urban centers. Because water is distributed unevenly, China's northern provinces, with a population of well over 400 million people, confront difficult choices. The signs of impending water stress can be seen in precipitously falling urban water tables and, to a lesser extent, rural water tables, the drying out of major rivers for several months of the year, the shrinkage of lake area by 15 percent, and severe water pollution, which renders almost 70 percent of the water unfit for use.[21] The situation is becoming steadily more critical, but it can be managed over the medium run through a combination of policies and structural changes. The structural changes relate principally to changes in sectoral shares—with services, the smallest users of water, expanding in size, industry remaining roughly constant, and agri-

---

19. In addition, China is entering into exploration and production contracts in Peru, Sudan, and Venezuela (Gallagher 2006).

20. The exception is the purchase of North Buzachi field in Kazakhstan by China National Petrochemical Corporation, but the estimated reserves are only 1.5 billion barrels (Nolan, Shipman, and Rui 2004). The 1,000-kilometer pipeline from Kazakhstan to Xinjiang is estimated to cost $3 billion ("China: Energy-led Foreign Policy" 2005; "In the Pipeline" 2004).

21. For details on the drying up of water tables, see World Bank (2001a, 2002a). Rivers dry up each year because the withdrawal of water upstream exceeds a safe level of about 55 percent. Between 2000 and 2004, the available supply of water fell by 13 percent ("China Water Shortage" 2006).

culture, currently the predominant consumer of water, shrinking relatively—and a shift in the product mix toward less-water-intensive products.

Three types of policies will have a large hand in determining the trend in water use in relation to GDP per capita or as a percentage of the population. First are policy incentives for developing technology that minimizes the water required for production (agricultural or industrial), reduces pollution, and reduces the costs of recycling. Second are policies that introduce stricter standards for household appliances and industrial equipment that contain use. Third are water-pricing policies aimed at limiting the growth of urban and irrigation demand for water. Such policies, if rigorously implemented, might be adequate for the foreseeable future. But under some long-term scenarios, it appears that a transfer of water from the Yangtze Basin to the northern rivers is needed.

Water Policy

The price of water is relatively low in China, even though water is far scarcer than in other countries. For instance, the price of water for farmers is almost negligible. This partly explains the large share of water used by the agricultural sector, even though the output per unit of water is as much as 70 times higher in industry than in low-valued yet water-intensive crops (Shalizi 2004). One ton of wheat valued at $200 requires 1,000 ton of water. The same amount of water can yield $14,000 if used by industry (Shalizi 2004), even though Chinese industry uses 2 to 10 times more water than comparable firms in other countries ("China: Water Shortages" 2001). One study estimates that importing 10 million tons of grains would save enough water to satisfy about half of the current shortage of water in the north (Murphy 2004). The price of water per cubic meter in urban areas was only $0.15 in 2003 compared with $0.47 in South Africa, $0.51 in the United States, and $1.45 in Germany (Shalizi 2004). The reutilization rate of water is also low in China: 30 percent compared with 75 percent in industrial countries ("China: Water Shortages" 2001).

Water shortage is most acute along the Yellow (Huang), Hai, and Huai (3-H) river basins. This area, with 8 percent of the water resources, is home to 460 million people, produces between half and two-thirds of China's major crops (see table 5.1), and accounts for a third of GDP (Gunaratnam 2004; Smil 2005).

Between 1989 and 1997, the municipal demand for water increased 34 percent, and the rural domestic demand for water increased 33 per-

Table 5.1. Agricultural Products Produced in the 3-H Basins as a Share of Total Output in China, 2001

Product	Percent of total output
Wheat	67
Corn	44
Millet	72
Peanuts	65
Sunflower	64
Sesame	50
Cotton	42

Source: Gunaratnam 2004.

cent. The urban population in the 3-H basins is projected to be 259 million people (48 percent urbanization) by 2020, up from the current population of 118 million (26 percent), mainly through migration. Even with implementation of demand management actions, there will be a large increase in municipal and industrial demand for water. A study conducted in 2001 notes, "In recent years the water flows through the deltas of the Hai and Yellow rivers have averaged about 15 BCM [billion cubic meters] less than the amount required to transport silt and maintain estuarine and coastal environments" (Shalizi 2004). In fact, between 1985 and 2000, the Yellow River dried up entirely in its lower reaches for several months in the year. Groundwater overexploitation in the Hai Basin is estimated to be 9 billion cubic meters annually. In water-scarce areas such as the 3-H basins, there will be a need for significant reductions in the amount of water used in irrigation, even after taking into account additional water transfers.

The problem needs to be tackled through better management of demand and, in the longer term, possibly geographic redistribution of people and water so as to increase the efficient use of this scarce resource. The limitations of supply are rendered more serious by pollution. One-third of the river waters in China are severely polluted, and almost three-quarters are polluted by industrial affluent and the nitrogenous compounds applied on the farms, thus reducing the effective supply of water. Better water treatment in urban areas and the reuse of water should be a priority (Shalizi 2004), and such reuse should be increased from the current 5 percent in urban areas and industry to 15 percent (Gunaratnam 2004).

One important step will be to build the institutions for assigning, enforcing, and trading water rights so as to enable water rights markets and the pricing mechanism to function better. However, these alone will not solve the problem. Better water measurement and volumetric water charging need to be implemented as well. Although water charges are quoted in terms of cubic meters of use, water is not measured adequately, and the usage charge typically is based on the average water use over an irrigated area, leading to the overuse of water (Gunaratnam 2004).[22] Without correctly measuring water usage, pricing policies will have minimal impact. Urban consumption will also need to be restrained by raising the price of water 10 percent yearly in real terms for the next 15 years in addition to the current proposed increase in water prices (Gunaratnam 2004; Henderson 2004b).[23]

Each of these actions will ease the supply constraints in the northern areas, but, in the absence of migration to more water-abundant areas, the fundamental imbalance between people and water resources will persist. This provides additional justification for encouraging greater interprovincial migration, proposed in chapter 3. Although water has been in short supply in the north, the distribution of population has not changed: 42 percent of the population lives in the north, which has only 14 percent of the water supply (Shalizi 2004).

China must use water more efficiently in order to realize its economic objectives at an affordable cost.[24] As with energy, the pricing issue needs to be addressed to encourage a more productive use of water. Even with the south-north transfer,[25] water use in irrigated agriculture in the 3-H basins will need to be reduced 20 billion to 28 billion cubic meters from present levels by 2020 (see table 5.2). In order to minimize socioeconomic consequences of this reduction, a major program to

22. Anecdotal evidence shows that, when water use is measured and priced correctly, farmers use much less water.

23. Since 1991, water prices have been raised eight times from the price of $0.02 per ton ("Water Rate Hikes" 2004). The price of water in Beijing in mid-2005 was Y4.5 per ton, and this low rate encourages inefficient use, which is depleting Beijing's underground aquifers. Annual consumption in Beijing is 3.5 billion cubic meters (Smil 2005). Current plans are to raise the price of water further.

24. China announced a water usage quota for dyeing, electric power, iron and steel, papermaking, and petroleum-refining industries in the hope of saving 6 billion tons of water a year. This was to be implemented in 2005. These industries account for two-thirds of industrial water use ("China: Water" 2003).

25. The capital costs of the south-north transfer of 18 billion cubic meters was estimated to be Y245 billion (World Bank 2001a). This scheme entails transferring 45 billion cubic meters of water from the Yangtze River, at a cost of $60 billion. The plan is to supply Beijing by 2007 and to complete the project by 2010 ("China: A Five-Year Outlook" 2004).

Table 5.2. Projected Availability of Water in the 3-H Basins under Three Scenarios of Growth in Demand, 2000–20
billion cubic meters a year

	6.5 percent growth			7.5 percent growth			8.5 percent growth		
	2000	2010	2020	2000	2010	2020	2000	2010	2020
Available water resources									
Surface water and groundwater	118	132	135	118	132	135	118	132	135
Transfer water	14	18	18	14	18	18	14	18	18
Water eliminated from available resources									
Additional water needed for the environment	0	15	15	0	15	15	0	15	15
Groundwater eliminated through overexploitation	0	9	9	0	9	9	0	9	9
Total water available for use	132	126	129	132	126	129	132	126	129
Water available for production									
Municipal and industrial demand (including demand management actions)	44	53	61	44	56	67	44	57	69
Irrigation	88	73	68	88	70	62	88	69	60

Source: Gunaratnam 2004; World Bank staff estimates.

increase the productivity of water in irrigated agriculture will be required, including measures to increase the agriculture yields per unit of water consumed and to shift cropping patterns to higher-value, less-water-intensive crops.

PART 3

Summing Up

CHAPTER 6

Connecting the Issues

As China enters into the Eleventh Plan, a number of development issues are beginning to crystallize, which will need to be addressed decisively in the second half of the decade by means of policies, many of which entail institutional changes. In this concluding section, we draw together these issues and briefly examine their interrelatedness and the implications.

Equitable Growth That Is Sustainable

Clearly, rapid growth must remain China's central economic objective in order to create the jobs that will raise living standards and further reduce poverty. In the face of falling labor elasticities in agriculture, manufacturing, and services, growth may need to be close to the average level for the past two decades if new entrants into the labor force and the unemployed are to be absorbed into well-paid jobs.[1] This will call for a balancing of policy efforts from two directions. One set of policies must spur efficiency and innovation so as to increase the contribution of productivity to growth and conserve scarce resources, especially energy and water.

---

1. The rate of absorption will also be determined by participation rates that, at 82 percent, are among the highest in the world (Brooks and Tao 2003).

Another set of policies needs to ensure a level of consumption and investment demand to support growth at the desired level, while maintaining macroeconomic balances and avoiding an overheating of the economy. Implementing and coordinating these two sets of policies will not be easy, but a strategy to promote rapid growth requires no less.

A large part of the gains in factor productivity will derive from the transfer of labor from the primary sector to large urban regions, which will require an effective removal of the remaining barriers to urban residence—the *hukou* system—and permit rural households to trade land leases. Migration could entail significant transitional problems for the cities receiving the influx. Uppermost will be the need to provide migrants with access to housing, health, and education services and a minimum social safety net that significantly improves on the current *dibao*. By providing social services and a safety net, cities could hold urban poverty in check. However, if the services are subsidized, the costs of providing them at preferential rates to both current urban residents and newcomers might exceed the fiscal resources of most cities. Some balance between user fees and tax-financed municipal subsidies will have to be struck, and this will be a major policy issue in the coming years.

If the gains in allocative efficiency and productivity are to be fully realized, urbanization strategy during the Eleventh Plan should ensure that urban agglomeration effects from the increasing size of cities reinforce the economy's growth momentum (Fujita and Thisse 2003), that pricing, technological, and institutional mechanisms are effectively deployed to contain water and energy intensity of GDP, and that rural areas derive full benefits from the remittances sent by migrants to their families, mainly through the postal network. Measures to conserve water and energy will also help to reduce the environmental costs of growth. By estimating "green GDP," China can keep closer track of how resource depletion and pollution are affecting development.

China's cities, in turn, will need to exploit the productivity gains from agglomeration which, as Scott puts it, "has a strong positive influence on the ability of cities to function as centers of learning, creativity, and innovation, for precisely because cities are constituted as dense transactions-intensive foci of many interdependent activities, they are also places in which new transactional encounters and experiences endlessly occur and in which enormous quantities of information are created and circulated daily. Large cities as a result are invariably important centers of resourcefulness and invention for all sectors of production" (Scott 2001, p. 819).

In other words, the metropolitan region provides the crucible within which innovative activity, which will be the touchstone for industrial competitiveness over the longer term, can flourish.

For urban agglomerations to fulfill their functions in the growth process, at least two other conditions need to be met. One is the capability of firms and financial institutions to rise to the challenge and become more efficient and innovative. The second is the integration of the national market, which links together the urban economic regions and exposes them to opportunities in the global economy.

The dynamism of the urban industrial economy will depend significantly on the ownership reform that imparts autonomy to China's medium and large manufacturing state-owned enterprises and banks. The next stage of reform entails privatizing the loss-making state-owned enterprises. This would enhance autonomy, which is vital if the management of firms is to maximize productivity and to build technological capability through greater investment in R&D. The government could support firms by investing in the national innovation system, in particular, tertiary education and research infrastructure. Autonomy for banks would, in turn, lead to better allocative outcomes and the availability of more financing for new entrants and private entities.

Ownership reform would accelerate domestic market integration because it would greatly weaken the motivation that local governments have for protecting firms and interfering with trade flows. It would also limit their capacity to pursue industrial policies using directed credit, which, in turn, would further improve the nationwide allocation of capital. By strengthening the legal institutions, the government could further buttress ownership reform, corporate governance of large firms, intellectual property rights over new technologies, and efforts to remove barriers to market integration.

Closing the Rural-Urban Welfare Gap

The urban engine of growth would boost the rural economy by generating demand and technological linkage effects, employment, and remittances. But rural welfare and poverty alleviation also require more direct intervention through measures to improve education, health, and infrastructure services and the safety net. Aggregate social indicators show that health and education standards in rural China are rising steadily, but these averages conceal wide divergences. In the poorest counties, gender differentials in education and access to health services persist, and a decline in public services is only partly offset by household purchase of services from private providers. Scattered evidence suggests that both the volume and the quality of publicly provided services is on the decline (or at the very least is not improving), and the quality of private health services is little better. This is reflected in the limited utility that rural students derive from education as well as an incidence of morbidity from accidents or chronic conditions that is not reflected in life expectancy data.

Social policy for the rural sector urgently requires strengthening through analysis of experience from across the country. However, based on the available findings, initially three types of interventions might be warranted:

- *Providing education and health services targeted to households in the poorest villages.* This could be achieved through suitably tailored fiscal arrangements that assign responsibilities and revenues to an administrative level that is organizationally equipped to deliver the services. Such services could enable poor households to climb out of poverty traps.
- *Analyzing the health profile of the rural population to determine the least-cost way of improving health status.* This might involve a mix of public and private interventions, with the mix varying from one part of the country to another. The interventions could combine a greater reliance on preventive medicine, in addition to strengthening actual service delivery to lower-income households. But the increased provision of publicly financed services by subnational governments is only one form of intervention. The creative use of new medical technologies and an effective melding of service delivery by public as well as private providers could yield the most benefits. And research on health care suggests that the gains from diminishing morbidity can be very large (Fogel 2004; Shine 2004).[2]
- *Launching nationwide efforts to prevent and treat HIV/AIDS and tuberculosis.* While the incidence of communicable diseases in China is lower than in other developing economies, the risks from the spread of HIV/AIDS and tuberculosis are rising and demand nationwide preventive efforts, together with more attention to the provision of palliative care. Poorer counties where the incidence of HIV or tuberculosis is on

---

2. The attention needs to be paid at an earlier stage. Fast growth during infancy is associated with obesity in later stages of life, often coupled with chronic ailments (Baird and others 2005).

the rise will not be able to cope without assistance from higher levels of government (Ahlburg and Flint 2001).

Implications of a Bigger Global Footprint

A rapidly growing and industrializing economy in which economic and physical well-being is widely shared will mean higher living standards throughout China. It also will have profound consequences for the rest of the world, and these must be factored into China's development strategy ("World Is Dancing" 2004). There are five channels through which China's development will impinge on her neighbors and the global economy.

First, China's export competitiveness and volume of exports will severely affect the trade prospects of other countries, not just in Asia but in other parts of the world as well.[3] Initially, China's competitive pressure will be strongest in consumer goods but is likely to spread to engineering products and services. Countries will need to adjust, strengthen their own technological capabilities, seek new specializations, and arrive at a new division of labor. Trade liberalization and China's manufacturing capability have greatly increased the competitiveness of the global trading environment, and, barring unforeseen developments, this will only intensify. There are benefits in this, but only for those countries— and firms—that are flexible and take strategic initiatives. In this context, it is unlikely that, in the medium term, the regional trading arrangements will significantly change the trading environment or provide much security to the weak performers. Nor is it apparent that East Asia as a region will move quickly toward much deeper institutional integration, although trading linkages will continue to evolve (Holst and Weiss 2004; Lincoln 2004; Low 2004). Already intraregional trade equals 53 percent of total trade. The region remains "culturally and socially diverse . . . [is] state centric, [is] characterized by unilateralism, has no fundamental identity or ideology, and is not ready for either deep economic integration or political convergence . . . Asian relationships are fundamentally strategic and pragmatic . . . The Asian way is to combine authoritarianism with the market" (Low 2004, pp. 7–8). However, this is changing, and the inexorable onward march of regional and global integration means that China and other countries must take account of the implica-

---

3. In the United States, manufacturers of products as diverse as machine tools, motherboards, furniture, and plastic molds have lost business to Chinese competitors, who can offer products of equivalent quality at a fraction of the price ("China Price" 2004).

tions of factor movements to coordinate policies in some areas. The signing of an ASEAN-China Free Trade Agreement on November 29, 2004, to reduce tariffs by 2010 underlined this perception of growing interdependence. The advantages of coordinating macro and health policies have been underscored by the crisis of 1997–8, the outbreak of SARS, and the threat of an avian flu epidemic.

Growth of the Chinese economy and integration of the domestic market will continue to serve as a magnet for FDI. Multinational companies faced with saturated or slowly growing markets in Europe, Japan, and the United States will continue to pour funds into China. How much this flow increases will depend on the steps taken to privatize and deregulate China's economy, define competition policy (and rules governing mergers and acquisitions), and substantially strengthen the legal and regulatory institutions and the enforcement of intellectual property rights. China's actions could spur similar institution-building efforts throughout the rest of Asia as well, because countries will have to compete harder for FDI by integrating more closely with the global economy.

Third, an expanding economy and rising FDI will greatly enlarge China's appetite for imports of commodities, intermediate components, machinery, and energy. This will help not only to stimulate the exports of the country's trading partners but also to make China far more reliant on the world economy.[4] This trend is evident throughout the world. How China manages this heightened dependence, especially for energy, will influence relations with China's neighbors and with the United States (Kemeny 2001; "Over a Barrel" 2004; "Quest for Energy" 2002). Partial insurance against an interruption in fuel supplies can be achieved by FDI in oil fields, long-term contracts, geographic diversification of sources, and reliance on multiple sources of energy. Some of these will require careful diplomacy but need not give rise to tensions. Investing in naval capability to project a position of power and protect vital sea lanes could, however, have longer-run ramifications and lead to an expensive arms race. How China seeks energy and feed grain security will have an important bearing on China's domestic investment, FDI, and international relations.

Fourth, as energy consumption grows, so will China's release of carbon and other greenhouse gases, which are impinging on the climate in East Asia and the world and whose effects will extend far into the future

---

4. Imports from ASEAN reached $47.3 billion in 2003, and exports to the region climbed to $31 billion ("Free Trade Pact" 2004).

(see table 6.1).[5] China is currently the second largest emitter of carbon, after the United States, accounting for 11 percent of global emissions in 2001 (Yang, Burnett, and Zhang 2001). In another decade, it could surpass the United States, given the trend in automobile use, the major role of metallurgical, chemical, construction materials, and engineering industries, and the rising household demand for electricity. This is a potentially worrisome development for China and for other countries. Although China's growth trend of carbon emissions cannot be halted, it could be moderated appreciably through a coordinated use of pricing and fuel-mix policies, technological leapfrogging, the setting of higher standards for appliances, autos, and equipment, and effective monitoring and enforcement measures (Lynch 2004).[6] The sooner such policies are implemented, the bigger the gains for China and the world, because climatic change will affect all.

Table 6.1. Carbon Dioxide Emissions in China, 1990–2003
teragram, unless otherwise noted

Year	Emissions
1990	2,405.0
2000	2,634.0
2001	2,742.0
2002	3,342.4
2003	3,958.0
Change (percent)	
2002–3	14.7
1990–2003	65

Source: Zittel and Treber 2004.
Note: A teragram is equal to 1 million tons.

---

5. The emission of carbon dioxide did not increase during 1996–9 due to accelerated structural change, especially the closure of inefficient state-owned enterprises. However, the trend of emissions is upward (Fisher-Vanden 2003; Wu, Kaneko, and Matsuoka 2005), and, between 2001 and 2002, carbon dioxide emissions grew 22 percent (Zittel and Treber 2003). During the twentieth century, average temperatures in East Asia increased 0.84 degrees Celsius. Simulation results for the twenty-first century suggest that temperatures in East Asia will rise 3–4 degrees Celsius, higher than the global rise, which will is projected to be 2–3 degrees Celsius (Zhao and Xu 2002). This will affect the availability of water and crop patterns in China. In particular, global warming will accentuate the water shortage in the 3-H basins and eventually reduce grain production in northern China (Wang 2002).
6. By encouraging the use of renewable energy, China could reduce carbon dioxide emissions 13 percent in 2010 (Yang, Burnett, and Zhang 2001).

Finally, other environmental spillovers must be taken into account. For example, China's demand for wood products could accelerate deforestation in Southeast Asia, with consequences that are both local and global.

The Next Decade for China and the World

Each of China's past five plans has posed its own challenges. During the Sixth Five-Year Plan starting in 1980, China embarked on the initial rounds of reform, starting with agricultural household contracting and the creation of special enterprise zones. The Seventh Plan saw the blossoming of product markets, fiscal decentralization, and a broadening of reforms to embrace the enterprise sector and trade. The Eighth Plan witnessed the start of a new round of changes following Deng Xiaoping's southern tour. With township and village enterprises and exports leading the way, China's industrial economy took off in the mid-1990s. This surge continued into the Ninth Plan, supported by further liberalization of markets, privatization of the smaller state-owned enterprises, and FDI. But the Ninth Plan also encountered another kind of challenge: the East Asian crisis. China managed to skirt the crisis without losing its growth momentum and entered the Tenth Plan on a strong note, with the WTO accession giving fresh impetus to trade, industrial, and financial reforms. During the period covered by the first five plans—1950–80—China's per capita GDP grew at an average rate of 4.0 percent. Between 1980 and 2000, it grew an average of close to 9 percent (Hu 2004).

Now with the Eleventh Plan, China faces yet more challenges and, given the scale of its economy (13 percent of global GDP), new responsibilities. The challenges are to make growth sustainable and more equitable, while keeping it at the highest level in the world.

The responsibility derives from China's changing role in the global economy. In 2004–5 the world depended on just two countries—China and the United States—for a significant share of total GDP growth. China's level of investment, demand for materials, foodstuffs, and energy, exports, carbon emissions, and appetite for FDI all have global implications. How China develops and performs during the Eleventh Plan will be of vital importance for China's people and for the world as a whole.

References

"1.46 billion by 2030s may hinder development." 2004. *China Daily.* October 25.

"The 11th Five-Year Plan for National Economy and Social Development," presented at The Fifth Plenary Session of the 16th Central Committee of the Communist Party of China (CPC), October 11, 2005. http://www.ccyl.org.cn/ywdd/files/ywdd20051019.htm (in Chinese).

Adams, James. 2002. "Comparative Localization of Academic and Industrial Spillovers." *Journal of Economic Geography* 2 (3): 253–78.

ADB (Asia Development Bank). 2004. *Poverty Profile of the People's Republic of China.* Manila.

Ahlburg, Dennis A., and Darla J. Flint. 2001. "Public Health Conditions and Policies in the Asia Pacific Region." *Asian-Pacific Economic Literature* 15 (2, November): 1–17.

Ahmad, Ehtishan, Raju Singh, and Benjamin Lockwood. 2004. "Taxation Reform and Changes in Revenue Assignments in China." IMF Working Paper WP/04/125. International Monetary Fund, Washington, DC.

Ahman, Max. 2006. "Government Policy and the Development of Electric Vehicles in Japan." *Energy Policy* 34 (4): 433–443.

Akin, John S., William H. Dow, and Peter M. Lance. 2004. "Did the Distribution of Health Insurance in China Continue to Grow Less Equitable in the Nineties? Results from a Longitudinal Survey." *Social Science and Medicine* 58 (2): 293–304.

Anderson, Kym, Jikun Huang, and Elena Ianchovichina. 2004. *Will China's WTO Accession Worsen Rural Poverty?* CEPR Discussion Paper 4196. London: Centre for Economic Policy Research.

"As Demand Grows, Jiangxi Copper Seeks Partner to Ensure Supply." 2004. *International Herald Tribune.* July 8.

"As Fleeting as Fashion." 2005. *Business China.* November 21.

Bai, Chong-En, Jiangyong Lu, and Zhigang Tao. 2005. "How Does Privatization Work in China?" Working Paper. Tsinghua University, Center for China in the World Economy, Beijing.

Baird, Janis, David Fisher, Patricia Lucas, Jos Kleijnen, Helen Roberts, and Catherine Law. 2005. "Being Big or Growing Fast: Systematic Review of Size and Growth in Infancy and Later Obesity." *British Medical Journal* 331 (October): 929–34.

Balcerowicz, Leszek. 2003. "Post-Communist Transition in a Comparative Perspective." Presented at Practitioners of Development Seminar Series, Washington, DC, November 18.

Baldwin, Richard E., and Philippe Martin. 2003. *Agglomeration and Regional Growth.* CEPR Discussion Paper 3960. London: Centre for Economic Policy Research.

Banerjee, Abhijit, Angus Deaton, and Esther Duflo. 2004. "Wealth, Health, and Health Services in Rural Rajasthan." *American Economic Review* 94 (2): 326–30.

Banerjee, Abhijit V., and Esther Duflo. 2003. "Inequality and Growth: What Can the Data Say?" *Journal of Economic Growth* 8 (3): 267–99.

Banister, Judith, and Kenneth Hill. 2004. "Mortality in China 1964–2000." *Population Studies* 58 (1): 55–75.

"Banking Sees Transformation." 2004. *Financial Times.* November 18.

Baumol, William J. 2002. *The Free Market Innovation Machine.* Princeton, NJ: Princeton University Press.

Beach, Marilyn. 2001. "Water, Pollution, and Public Health in China." *Lancet* 358 (November): 735.

Bhalla, A. S., and Shufang. Qiu. 2002. *China's Accession to WTO: Its Impact on Chinese Employment.* UNCTAD Discussion Paper 163. Geneva, Switzerland: United Nations Conference on Trade and Development.

Bielke, Audra. 2004. "Illegal Migration in China and Implications for Governance." *In the National Interest* 3 (26, June). http://www. inthenationalinterest.com/Articles/Vol3Issue26/Vol3Issue26Bielke.html.

Bird, Richard M. 2004. "Getting It Right: Financing Urban Development in China." Prepared for the Eleventh Five-Year Plan of China. World Bank, Washington, DC.

Blalock, Garrick, and Paul Gertler. 2003. "Technology Acquisition in Indonesian Manufacturing: The Effect of Foreign Direct Investment." Background paper prepared for "Innovative East Asia" Study. World Bank, Washington, DC.

Blanchard, Olivier, and Michael Kremer. 1997. "Disorganization." *Quarterly Journal of Economics* 112 (4): 1091–1126.

Blomstrom, Magnus, and Ari Kokko. 2003. "The Economics of Foreign Direct Investment Incentives." NBER Working Paper 9489. National Bureau of Economic Research, Cambridge, MA.

Bloom, David E., and Jeffrey G. Williamson. 1997. "Demographic Transitions and Economic Miracles in Emerging Asia." NBER Working Paper 6268. National Bureau of Economic Research, Cambridge, MA.

Boucher, Steve, Oded Stark, and J. Edward Taylor. 2005. "A Gain with a Drain? Evidence from Rural Mexico on the New Economics of the Brain Drain." ARE Working Paper 05-005. Department of Agriculture and Resource Economics, University of California, Davis.

BP. 2005. *Statistical Review of World Energy 2005*. London: BP.

Brajer, Victor, and Robert W. Mead. 2004. "Valuing Air Pollution Mortality in China's Cities." *Urban Studies* 41 (8): 1567–85.

Bresnahan, Timothy F., Alfonso Gambardella, and AnnaLee Saxenian. 2001. "'Old Economy' Inputs for 'New Economy' Outcomes: Cluster Formation in the New Silicon Valleys." *Industrial and Corporate Change* 10 (4): 835–60.

Brooks, Ray, and Ran Tao. 2003. "China's Labor Market Performance and Challenges." IMF Working Paper WP/03/210. International Monetary Fund, Washington, DC.

Burns, John P. 2003. "'Downsizing' the Chinese State: Government Retrenchment in the 1990s." *China Quarterly* 175 (September): 775–802.

Cai, Fang, ed. 2001. *Zhongguo Renkou Liudong Fangshi Yu Tujing (1990–1999 Nian) [The Means and Paths of Population Migration in China (1990–1999)]*. Beijing: Shehui kexue wenxian chubanshe [Social Science Documentation Publishing House].

Cai, Fang, and Dewen Wang. 2003. "Migration as Marketization: What Can We Learn from China's 2000 Census Data?" *China Review* 3 (2): 73–93.

Calderón, César, and Alberto Chong. 2004. "Volume and Quality of Infrastructure and the Distribution of Income: An Empirical Investigation." *Review of Income and Wealth* 50 (1): 87–106.

Campos, Nauro F., and Fabrizio Coricelli. 2002. "Growth in Transition: What We Know, What We Don't, and What We Should." *Journal of Economic Literature* 40 (September): 793–836.

Cao, Cong. 2004. "Chinese Science and the 'Nobel Prize Complex'." *Minerva* 42 (1): 151–72.

Cao, Jing-chun. 2001. "Guanyu Lanyin Hukou Wenti Di Sikao [Some Thoughts on the Blue Stamp Hukou]." *Population and Economics* 6: 15–21, 66.

"The Cauldron Boils." 2005. *The Economist*. October 1.

Chan, Kam Wing. 1998. "Recent Migration in Mainland China: Impacts and Policy Issues." *Journal of Population Studies* 19 (October): 33–52.

Chang, Chun, Belton M. Fleisher, and Elliott Parker. 2001. "The Impact of China's Entry into the WTO: Overview." *China Economic Review* 11 (4): 319–442.

Chen, Tain-Jy, and Ying-Hua Ku. 2003. "The Effect of Overseas Investment on Domestic Employment." NBER Working Paper 10156. National Bureau of Economic Research, Cambridge, MA.

Chen, Yangle. 2001. "The Studies of Scale of the Chinese Surplus Agricultural Labor Force and the Economic Price of Its Being Detained." *Population and Economics* 2: 52–58.

Cheng, Leonard K., and Yum K. Kwan. 2000. "What Are the Determinants of the Location of Foreign Direct Investment? The Chinese Experience." *Journal of International Economics* 51 (2): 379–400.

Cheung, Kui-yin, and Ping Lin. 2004. "Spillover Effects of FDI on Innovation in China: Evidence from the Provincial Data." *China Economic Review* 15 (1): 25–44.

Cheung, Richard C., T. C. Chu, and Jacques Penhirin. 2002. "Wholesale Moves in China." *McKinsey Quarterly* 3.

"China Backs Foreigner's Investments in Banks." 2005. *Financial Times.* December 6.

"China Broadens Quest for Energy." 2004. *International Herald Tribune.* November 24.

"China Continues to Fill up on Oil, but Pace Slackens." 2005. *Wall Street Journal.* October 9.

"China Eases Rules Binding People to Birth Regions." 2001. *New York Times.* October 23.

"China May Triple Planned Oil Reserve." 2004. *Asian Wall Street Journal.* November 26.

China Population Census Office 1982. *1982 Population Census of China.* Beijing: China Statistics Press.

———. 2002. *Tabulation on the 2000 Population Census on the People's Republic of China.* Beijing: China Statistics Press.

"The China Price." 2004. *Business Week.* December 6.

"China Sees Role for Foreign Suppliers in Meeting Atomic Energy Targets." 2004. *Financial Times.* September 2.

"China Taking." 2004. http://umbc7.umbc.edu/~earickso/Bobsweb/pages/ Green_GDP.html.

"China: Capacity Expansion to End Power Shortage." 2004. *Oxford Analytica.* March 29.

"China: Energy-led Foreign Policy Raises the Stakes." 2005. *Oxford Analytica.* January 27.

"China: A Five-Year Outlook." 2004. *Oxford Analytica* in association with Oxford Economic Forecasting, London.

"China: High Oil Prices Force Policy Movement." 2005. *Oxford Analytica.* October 3.

"China: 'Hukou' System under Strain." 2006. *Oxford Analytica.* January 16.

"China: Interest Reforms Set Stage for Currency Change." 2004. *Oxford Analytica.* November 8.

"China: Report Points to Urban Divide." 2006. *Oxford Analytica.* February 7.

"China: Soaring Exports Will Fuel Criticism." 2006. *Oxford Analytica.* January 17.

"China: Strategic Oil Reserve." 2003. *Oxford Analytica.* February 26.

"China: Surging Oil Demand Changes Energy Scene." 2004. *Oxford Analytica.* February 26.

"China: Towards 'Xiaokang,' But Still Living Dangerously." 2004. *Lancet.* February 7.

"China: Trade Boom Poses Threats and Opportunities." 2004. *Oxford Analytica.* July 14.

"China, US Sign Three-Year Pact on Textile Trade." 2005. *Wall Street Journal.* October 9.

"China: Water." 2003. *Business China.* January 20.

"China: Water Shortage Poses Significant Risks." 2006. *Oxford Analytica.* February 13.

"China: Water Shortages." 2001. *Oxford Analytica.* November 1.

"China's Challenges: Health and Wealth." 2006. *Lancet.* February 25.

"China's 'Green GDP' Index Facing Technological Problem, Local Protectionism." 2004. *People's Daily.* April 3.

"China's Railways Lined up for Listing." 2005. *Financial Times.* November 1.

"China's Rural Healthcare Crisis: Forward to the Past." 1999. *Business China.* November 22.

"China's Trade Surplus Widens to Nine-Year High." 2005. *Financial Times.* January 11.

"Chronic Overinvestment, Excess Supply, and Endemic Corruption." 2003. *Financial Times.* September 23.

Claeson, Mariam, Hong Wang, and Shanlian Hu. 2004. "A Critical Review of Public Health in China." Working Paper. World Bank, Washington, DC.

"Clean Machine." 2004. *Economist.* September 2.

Connelly, Rachel, and Zhenzhen Zheng. 2003. "Determinants of School Enrollment and Completion of 10 to 18 Year Olds in China." *Economics of Education Review* 22 (4): 379–88.

Cornelius, Peter, and Jonathan Story. 2005. "China Revolutionizes Energy Markets." *Far Eastern Economic Review* 168 (9, October): 21–24.

Cornillie, Jan, and Samuel Fankhauser. 2004. "The Energy Intensity of Transition Countries." *Energy Economics* 26 (3): 283–95.

"Cotton in China: Soft Landing?" 2004. *Economist*. July 3.

"Cut-Throat Competition in China Keeps Foreign Companies' Earnings at Low Level." 2004. *Financial Times*. December 6.

Dabla-Norris, Era. 2004. "Issues in Intergovernmental Fiscal Relations in China." Paper prepared for the Report on Eleventh Five-Year Plan. World Bank, Washington, DC.

Dacosta, Maria, and Wayne Carroll. 2001. "Township and Village Enterprises, Openness, and Regional Economic Growth in China." *Post-Communist Economies* 13 (2): 229–41.

Davis, Mike. 2004. "Planet of Slums." *New Left Review* 26 (March-April): 5–54.

de Brauw, Alan, and Scott Rozelle. 2002. "Reconciling the Returns to Education in Rural China." University of California, Davis.

Demurger, Sylvie. 2001. "Infrastructure Development and Economic Growth: An Explanation for Regional Disparities in China?" *Journal of Comparative Economics* 29 (1): 95–117.

"Desertification Damage." 2002. *Oxford Analytica*. August 29.

DFID (U.K. Department for International Development). 2004. *China Urban Poverty Study*. Report Contract CNTR 04 5394. London: DFID.

"Dissecting China's Middle Stratum." 2004. *China Daily*. October 27.

Dong, Hengjin. 2003. "Health Financing Policies: Patient Care-Seeking Behavior in Rural China." *International Journal of Technology Assessment in Health Care* 19 (3): 526–32.

Downs, Anthony. 2004. *Still Stuck in Traffic: Coping with Peak-Hour Traffic Congestion*. Washington, DC: Brookings Institution Press.

"The Dragon and the Eagle." 2004. *Economist*. October 2.

"Driven by the Oil Price." 2004. *Economist*. April 28.

Du, Shufa, Tom A. Mroz, Fengying Zhai, and Barry M. Popkin. 2004. "Rapid Income Growth Adversely Affects Diet Quality in China—Particularly for the Poor!" *Social Science and Medicine* 59 (7): 1505–15.

Du, Yang, Albert Park, and Sangui Wang. 2005. "Migration and Rural Poverty in China." *Journal of Comparative Economics* 33 (4): 688–709.

East Asia Economic Review, January 17, 2005.

Easterly, William, Michael Kremer, Lant Pritchett, and Lawrence H. Summers. 1993. "Good Policy or Good Luck? Country Growth Performance and Temporary Shocks." *Journal of Monetary Economics* 32 (3): 459–83.

Eberhardt, Markus, Julie McLaren, Andrew Millington, and Barry Wilkinson. 2004. "Multiple Forces in Component Localisation in China." *European Management Journal* 22 (3): 290–303.

Economist Intelligence Unit. 2004. "Country Report China." Economist Intelligence Unit, London, December.

Eichengreen, Barry. 2004. "Hanging Together? On Monetary and Financial Cooperation." In Shahid Yusuf, M. Anjum Altaf, and Kaoru Nabeshima, eds.,

Global Change and East Asian Policy Initiatives. New York: Oxford University Press.

Eichengreen, Barry, Yeongseop Rhee, and Hui Tong. 2004. "The Impact of China on the Exports of Other Asian Countries." NBER Working Paper 10768. National Bureau of Economic Research, Cambridge, MA.

Ekboir, Javier, ed. 2002. *CIMMYT 2000–2001 World Wheat Overview and Outlook: Developing No-Till Packages for Small-Scale Farmers.* Mexico, DF: International Maize and Wheat Improvement Center (CIMMYT).

Elbers, Chris, Tomoki Fujii, Peter Lanjouw, Berk Ozler, and Wesley Yin. 2004. "Poverty Alleviation through Geographic Targeting: How Much Does Disaggregation Help?" Policy Research Working Paper 3419. World Bank, Washington, DC.

"Energy Conservation to Top Government Agenda." 2004. *China Daily.* July 5.

"Environmental Degradation Carries Costs for All." 2005. *Oxford Analytica.* March 24.

"Faintly Declining Investment." 2005. *Economist.* October 27.

Fan, C. Cindy. 2004a. "Addition to Note: Impacts of Removal of Migration Restrictions." Prepared for the Eleventh Five-Year Plan of China. World Bank, Washington, DC.

———. 2004b. "Migration in China: A Review of Recent Findings and Policy Recommendations." Prepared for the Eleventh Five-Year Plan of China. World Bank, Washington, DC.

Fan, Shenggen, Linxiu Zhang, and Xiaobo Shang. 2002. *Growth, Inequality, and Poverty in Rural China: The Role of Public Investments.* IFPRI Research Report 125. International Food Policy Research Institute, Washington, DC.

Fan, Shenggen, and Xiaobo Zhang. 2004. "Infrastructure and Regional Economic Development in Rural China." *China Economic Review* 15 (2): 203–14.

FAO (Food and Agriculture Organization). 2003. *Selected Indicators of Food and Agriculture Development in Asia-Pacific Region: 1992–2002.* Food and Agriculture Organization of the United Nations, Regional Office for Asia and the Pacific, Bangkok, Thailand.

FAS (Federation of American Scientists). 2003. *Degraded Lands of China; Problems and Opportunities.* Washington, DC: FAS.

FIAS (Foreign Investment Advisory Service). 2003. "Latvia: Toward a Knowledge Economy: Upgrading the Investment Climate and Enhancing Technology Transfer." Mimeo. International Finance Corporation, Washington, DC.

Fisher-Vanden, Karen. 2003. "The Effects of Market Reforms on Structural Change: Implications for Energy Use and Carbon Emissions in China." *Energy Journal* 24 (3): 27–62.

Fisher-Vanden, Karen, Gary H. Jefferson, Hongmei Liu, and Quan Tao. 2004. "What Is Driving China's Decline in Energy Intensity?" *Resource and Energy Economics* 26 (1): 77–97.

"Five More Years." 2005. *Economist*. October 15.

Florida, Richard. 2000. "Competing in the Age of Talent: Quality of Place and the New Economy." Carnegie Mellon University, Pittsburg.

————. 2002. *The Rise of the Creative Class: And How It's Transforming Work, Leisure, Community, and Everyday Life.* New York: Basic Books.

Fogel, Robert W. 2004. "High-Performing Asian Economies." NBER Working Paper 10752. National Bureau of Economic Research, Cambridge, MA.

"Free Trade Pact with ASEAN in Sight." 2004. *China Daily.* October 22.

Fujita, Kuniko, and Richard Child Hill. 2005. "Innovative Tokyo." Policy Research Working Paper 3507. World Bank, Washington, DC.

Fujita, Masahisa, and Jacques-François Thisse. 2003. "Does Geographical Agglomeration Foster Economic Growth? And Who Gains and Loses from It?" *Japanese Economic Review* 54 (2): 121–45.

Fujita, Masahisa, Tomoya Mori, J. Vernon Henderson, and Yoshitsugu Kanemoto. 2004. "Spatial Distribution of Economic Activities in Japan and China." In J. Vernon Henderson and Jacques-François Thisse, eds., *Handbook of Regional and Urban Economics.* Amsterdam: North Holland.

"The Future Is Clean." 2004. *Economist*. September 2.

"The Future's a Gas." 2004. *Economist*. April 28.

Gallagher, Kelly Sims. 2006. "Limits to Leapfrogging in Energy Technology? Evidence from the Chinese Automobile Industry." *Energy Policy* 34 (4, March): 383–94.

Gao, Jun, Shenglan Tang, Rachel Tolhurst, and Keqing Rao. 2001. "Changing Access to Health Services in Urban China: Implications for Equity." *Health Policy and Planning* 16 (3): 302–12.

"The Geologic of China's Oil." 1979. *Economist*. March 3.

Gilbert, John, Robert Scollay, and Bijit Bora. 2004. "New Regional Trading Developments in the Asia-Pacific Region." In Shahid Yusuf, M. Anjum Altaf, and Kaoru Nabeshima, eds., *Global Change and East Asian Policy Initiatives.* New York: Oxford University Press.

Giles, John, Emily Hannum, Albert Park, and Juwei Zhang. 2003. "Life-Skills, Schooling, and the Labor Market in Urban China: New Insights from Adult Literacy Measurement." Working Paper Series 2003-21. International Centre for the Study of East Asian Development, Kitakyushu, Japan.

Gilley, Bruce. 2004. *China's Democratic Future: How It Will Happen and Where It Will Lead.* New York: Columbia University Press.

Glaeser, Edward L., and Jesse Shapiro. 2001. "Is There a New Urbanism? The Growth of U.S. Cities in the 1990s." NBER Working Paper w8357. National Bureau of Economic Research, Cambridge, MA.

Glomsrod, Solveig, and Taoyuan Wei. 2005. "Coal Cleaning: A Viable Strategy for Reduced Carbon Emissions and Improved Environment in China?" *Energy Policy* 33 (4): 525–42.

Gnansounou, Edgard, and Jun Dong. 2004. "Opportunity for Inter-Regional Integration of Electricity Markets: The Case of Shandong and Shanghai in East China." *Energy Policy* 32 (15): 1737–51.

Görg, Holger. 2005. "Fancy a Stay at the 'Hotel California'? The Role of Easy Entry and Exit for FDI." *Kyklos* 58 (4): 519–35.

Goldberg, Linda. 2004. "Financial-Sector FDI and Host Countries: New and Old Lessons." NBER Working Paper 10441. National Bureau of Economic Research, Cambridge, MA.

González-Páramo, and Pablo Hernández De Cos. 2005. "The Impact of Public Ownership and Competition on Productivity." *Kyklos* 58 (4): 495–517.

"Gouged." 2005. *Economist*. November 19.

"Go West, Westerners." 2005. *Business Week*. November 14.

Gunaratnam, Daniel. 2004. "China: Water Resources Issues and Proposed Strategy." Paper prepared for the Report on Eleventh Five-Year Plan. World Bank, Washington, DC.

Gustafsson, Bjorn, and Shi Li. 2004. "Expenditures on Education and Health Care and Poverty in Rural China." *China Economic Review* 15 (3): 292–301.

Gwatkin, Davidson R., Abbas Bhuiya, and Cesar G. Victora. 2004. "Making Health Systems More Equitable." *Lancet* 364 (October): 1273–80.

Hallock, John L. Jr., Pradeep J. Tharakan, Charles A. S. Hall, Michael Jefferson, and Wei Wu. 2004. "Forecasting the Limits to the Availability and Diversity of Global Conventional Oil Supply." *Energy* 29 (11): 1673–96.

Haskel, Jonathan E., Sonia C. Pereira, and Matthew J. Slaughter. 2002. "Does Inward Foreign Direct Investment Boost the Productivity of Domestic Firms?" NBER Working Paper 8724. National Bureau of Economic Research, Cambridge, MA.

Hausmann, Ricardo, Lant Pritchett, and Dani Rodrik. 2004. "Growth Accelerations." NBER Working Paper w8952. National Bureau of Economic Research, Cambridge, MA, May.

Havrylyshyn, Oleh. 2004. "Avoid Hubris but Acknowledge Successes: Lessons from the Postcommunist Transition." *Finance and Development* 41 (3, September): 38–41.

Heckman, James J. 2003. "China's Investment in Human Capital." *Economic Development and Cultural Change* 51 (4, July): 795–804.

Held, David, Anthony McGrew, David Goldblatt, and Jonathan Perraton. 1999. *Global Transformations: Politics, Economics, and Culture*. Palo Alto, CA: Stanford University Press.

Henderson, J. Vernon. 2004a. "Issues Concerning Urbanization in China." Prepared for the Eleventh Five-Year Plan of China. World Bank, Washington, DC.

———. 2004b. "Scenarios Concerning Urban Growth." Paper prepared for the Report on Eleventh Five-Year Plan. World Bank, Washington, DC.

Hertel, Thomas, and Fan Zhai. 2004. "Labor Market Distortions, Rural-Urban Inequality, and the Opening of China's Economy." Policy Research Working Paper 3455. World Bank, Washington, DC.

Heytens, Paul, and Harm Zebregs. 2003. "How Fast Can China Grow?" In Wanda Tseng and Markus Rodlauer, eds., *China: Competing in the Global Economy.* Washington, DC: International Monetary Fund.

Hines, James R. 1996. "Altered States: Taxes and the Location of Foreign Direct Investment in America." *American Economic Review* 86 (5): 1076–94.

Ho, Samuel P. S., and George C. S. Lin. 2003. "Emerging Land Markets in Rural and Urban China: Policies and Practices." *China Quarterly* 175 (September): 681–707.

Hofman, Bert, and Susana Cordeiro Guerra. 2004. "Ensuring Inter-Regional Equity and Poverty Reduction." In *Managing Decentralization in East Asia.* Washington, DC: World Bank.

Holst, David Roland, and John Weiss. 2004. "ASEAN and China: Export Rivals or Partners in Regional Growth?" *World Economy* 27 (8, August): 1255–74.

Holz, Carsten A. 2006. "Why China's New GDP Data Matters." *Far Eastern Economic Review* 169 (1): 54–57.

Honohan, Patrick. 2004. "Finance in China: Removing Ambiguity over Government's Role." Paper prepared for the Report on Eleventh Five-Year Plan. World Bank, Washington, DC.

Hsiao, Frank S. T., and Mei-Chu Hsiao. 2004. "The Chaotic Attractor of Foreign Direct Investment: Why China? A Panel Data Analysis." *Journal of Asian Economics* 15 (4): 641–70.

Hu, Angang 2004. *China: New Development Strategy.* Hangzhou: Zhejiang People's Publishing Press.

Huang, Jikun, Ruifa Hu, Hans van Meijl, and Frank van Tongeren. 2004. "Biotechnology Boosts to Crop Productivity in China: Trade and Welfare Implications." *Journal of Development Economics* 75 (1): 27–54.

Huang, Jikun, Ninghui Li, and Scott Rozelle. 2003. "Trade Reform, Household Effects, and Poverty in Rural China." *American Journal of Agricultural Economics* 85 (5): 1292–98.

Huang, Jikun, Scott Rozelle, and Min Chang. 2003. "Tracking the Nature of Distortion to Agricultural Price: The Case of China and Its Accession to the WTO." Working Paper. University of California, Davis.

Huang, Yasheng. 2001a. "Why Chinese Firms Stay at Home." *Project Syndicate.* December.

———. 2001b. "Why Overseas Chinese Dominate China's Exports." *Project Syndicate.* June.

Huang, Yasheng, and Wenhua Di. 2004. "A Tale of Two Provinces: The Institutional Environment and Foreign Ownership in China." Mimeo. Massachusetts Institute of Technology, Cambridge, MA.

Hubert, Florence, and Nigel Pain. 2002. "Fiscal Incentives, European Integration, and the Location of Foreign Direct Investment." *Manchester School* 70 (3): 336–63.

Hufbauer, Gary Clyde, and Yee Wong. 2004. "China Bashing 2004." International Economics Policy Briefs PB04-5 (September). International Institute for Economics, Washington, DC.

"In Face of Rural Unrest, China Rolls out Reforms." 2006. *Washington Post*. January 28.

"In the Pipeline." 2004. *Economist*. May 1.

Incandela, Denise, Kathleen L. McLaughlin, and Christiana Smith Shi. 1999. "Retailers to the World." *McKinsey Quarterly* 3: 84–97.

"Interior Has Strategic Role in Competitiveness." 2004. *Oxford Analytica*. November 16.

International Rice Research Institute. Various years. World Rice Statistics database. Manila, Philippines.

"International: China Textile Talks Stall." 2005. *Oxford Analytica*. September 2.

"International: Developing World Generates FDI Outflows." 2004. *Oxford Analytica*. August 26.

"International: Metal Supply Hitting Critical Levels." 2004. *Oxford Analytica*. September 14.

"International: Prices to Rise as Copper Stocks Halve." 2004. *Oxford Analytica*. September 15.

"Iron Deficiency." 2003. *Far Eastern Economic Review*. October 9.

Ito, Junichi. 2002. *Why TVEs Have Contributed to Interregional Imbalances in China*. EPTD Discussion Paper 91. Washington, DC: International Food Policy Research Institute.

Javorcik, Beata Smarzynska. 2004. "Does Foreign Direct Investment Increase the Productivity of Domestic Firms? In Search of Spillovers through Backward Linkages." *American Economic Review* 94 (3): 605–27.

Jiang, Zemin. 2002. "Build a Well-off Society in an All-Round Way and Create a New Situation in Building Socialism with Chinese Characteristics," delivered at the 16th National Congress of the Communist Party of China (CPC) on Nov. 8, 2002. http://news.xinhuanet.com/english/2002-11/18/content_633685.htm.

Jiangsu Municipal Statistics Bureau. 2005. *Jiangsu Statistical Yearbook 2005*. Beijing: China Statistics Press.

Jin, Songqing, Jikun Huang, Ruifa Hu, and Scott Rozelle. 2002. "The Creation and Spread of Technology and Total Factor Productivity in China's Agriculture." *American Journal of Agricultural Economics* 84 (4): 916–30.

Johnson, D. Gale. 2003. "Provincial Migration in China in the 1990s." *China Economic Review* 14 (1): 22–31.

Jorgenson, Dale and Khuong Vu. 2005 "Information Technology and the World Economy." *Scandinavian Journal of Economics.* 107 (4): 631–650.

Judson, Horace Freeland. 2005. "China's Great Experiment." *Technology Review.* 108 (11): 52–61.

Kan, Haidong, and Bingheng Chen. 2004. "Particulate Air Pollution in Urban Areas of Shanghai, China: Health-Based Economic Assessment." *Science of the Total Environment* 322 (1-3): 71–79.

Kanbur, Ravi. 1996. "Income Distribution and Development." Working Paper. Cornell University, Ithaca, NY.

Kanbur, Ravi, and Xiaobo Zhang. 2001. "Fifty Years of Regional Inequality in China: A Journey through Revolution, Reform, and Openness." Cornell University, Ithaca, NY; CEPR (Centre for Economic Policy Research), London; IFPRI (International Food Policy Research Institute), Washington, DC.

————. 2003. *Spatial Inequality in Education and Health Care in China.* CEPR Discussion Paper 4136. London: Centre for Economic Policy Research.

Katz, Michael L., and Howard A. Shelanski. 2004. "Merger Policy and Innovation: Must Enforcement Change to Account for Technological Change?" NBER Working Paper 10710. National Bureau of Economic Research, Cambridge, MA.

Keller, Wolfgang. 2002. "Geographic Localization of International Technology Diffusion." *American Economic Review* 92 (1): 120–42.

Keller, Wolfgang, and Stephen R. Yeaple. 2003. "Multinational Enterprises, International Trade, and Productivity Growth: Firm-Level Evidence from the United States." NBER Working Paper 9504. National Bureau of Economic Research, Cambridge, MA.

Kemeny, Leslie G. 2001. "Energy in the Asian-Pacific Region." *Asian-Pacific Economic Literature* 15 (1): 1–12.

Keng, C. W. Kenneth. 2006. "China's Unbalanced Economic Growth." *Journal of Contemporary China* 15 (46): 182–214.

Khaleghian, Peyvand. 2004. "Public Management and the Essential Public Health Functions." Mimeo. World Bank, Washington, DC.

Kodama, Fumio, and Jun Suzuki. 2005. "How Japanese Companies Brought New Sciences for Restructuring Their Businesses: Characterizing Receiver-Active National System of Innovation." Presented at the Conference on University Industry Linkages in Metropolitan Areas in Asia, Washington, DC, November 17.

Konings, Jozef, Patrick van Cayseele, and Frederic Warzynski. 2005. "The Effects of Privatization and Competitive Pressure on Firms' Price-Cost Margins: Micro Evidence from Emerging Economies." *Review of Economics and Statistics* 87 (1): 124–34.

Krumm, Kathie, and Homi Kharas. 2004. "Overview." In Kathie Krumm and Homi Kharas, eds., *East Asia Integrates.* Washington, DC: World Bank.

Krusekopf, Charles C. 2002. "Diversity in Land-Tenure Arrangements under the Household Responsibility System in China." *China Economic Review* 13 (2-3): 297–312.

Kuijs, Louis, and Tao Wang. 2005. "China's Pattern of Growth: Moving to Sustainability and Reducing Inequality." Policy Research Working Paper 3767. World Bank, Washington, DC.

Lall, Sanjaya, and Manuel Albaladejo. 2004. "China's Competitive Performance: A Threat to East Asian Manufactured Exports?" *World Development* 32 (9): 1441–66.

Lane, Kevin P., and Ian St-Maurice. 2006. "The Chinese Consumer: To Spend or to Save?" *McKinsey Quarterly* 1.

Lange, Glenn-Marie. 2003. *Policy Applications of Environmental Accounting.* Environmental Economics Series 88. Washington, DC: World Bank.

Lardy, Nicholas R. 2002. *Integrating China into the Global Economy.* Washington, DC: Brookings Institution.

Larson, Eric D., Zhongxin Wu, Pat DeLaquil, Wenying Chen, and Pengfei Gao. 2003. "Future Implications of China's Energy-Technology Choices." *Energy Policy* 31 (12): 1189–204.

Leamer, Edward E., and Michael Storper. 2001. "The Economic Geography of the Internet Age." *Journal of International Business Studies* 32 (4): 641–65.

Lee, Kuan Yew. 2005. "India in an Asian Renaissance." Presented at the 37th Jawaharlal Nehru Memorial Lecture, New Delhi, India, November 21.

Lewis, Maureen, Gunnar Eskeland, and Ximena Traa-Valerezo. 2004. "Primary Health Care in Practice: Is It Effective?" *Health Policy* 70 (3): 303–25.

Li, Yuefen. 2002. *China's Accession to WTO: Exaggerated Fears?* UNCTAD Discussion Paper 165. Geneva, Switzerland: United Nations Conference on Trade and Development.

Li, Zhi Dong. 2003. "An Econometric Study on China's Economy, Energy, and Environment to Year 2030." *Energy Policy* 31 (11): 1137–50.

Lim, Ewe-Ghee. 2001. "Determinants of, and the Relation between, Foreign Direct Investment and Growth: A Summary of the Recent Literature." IMF Working Paper WP/01/175. International Monetary Fund, Washington, DC.

Lim, Meng-Kin, Hui Yang, Tuohong Zhang, Zijun Zhou, Wen Feng, and Yude Chen. 2004. "China's Evolving Health Care Market: How Doctors Feel and What They Think." *Health Policy* 69 (3): 329–37.

Lin, Justin Yifu, and Zhiqiang Liu. 2000. "Fiscal Decentralization and Economic Growth in China." *Economic Development and Cultural Change* 49 (1): 1–21.

Lincoln, Edward J. 2004. *East Asian Economic Regionalism.* Washington, DC: Brookings Institution.

Lindert, Peter H. 1999. "The Bad Earth? China's Soils and Agricultural Development since the 1930s." *Economic Development and Cultural Change* 47 (4, July): 701–36.

Liu, Gordon, Brian Nolan, and Chen Wen. 2004. "Urban Health Insurance and Financing in China." Working Paper. World Bank, Washington, DC.

Liu, Xiaohui, and Chenggang Wang. 2003. "Does Foreign Direct Investment Facilitate Technological Progress? Evidence from Chinese Industries." *Research Policy* 32 (6): 945–53.

Liu, Xiaming, Chengang Wang, and Yingqi Wei. 2001. "Causal Links between Foreign Direct Investment and Trade in China." *China Economic Review* 12 (2-3): 190–202.

Liu, Yuanli, William C. Hsiao, and Karen Eggleston. 1999. "Equity in Health and Health Care: The Chinese Experience." *Social Science and Medicine* 49 (10): 1349–56.

Liu, Yunhua and Xiaobing Wang. 2005. "Technological Progress and Chinese Agricultural Growth in the 1990s." *China Economic Review* 16 (4): 419–40.

Lloyd, Peter, Kerrin Vautier, and Paul Crampton. 2004. "Harmonizing Competition Policies." In Shahid Yusuf, M. Anjum Altaf, and Kaoru Nabeshima, eds., *Global Change and East Asian Policy Initiatives.* New York: Oxford University Press.

Low, Linda. 2004. "A Comparative Evaluation and Prognosis of Asia Pacific Bilateral and Regional Trade Arrangements." *Asian-Pacific Economic Literature* 18 (1, May): 1–11.

Lynch, Michael C. 2004. "A Review of Expectations for Long-Term Energy." *Journal of Energy Literature* 10 (1, June): 3–21.

Ma, Guoan. 2001. "Population Migration and Crime in a Changing China." In Jianhong Liu, Lening Zhang, and Steven F. Messner, eds., *Crime and Social Control in a Changing China.* Westport, CT: Greenwood Publishing Group.

"Made in China." 2005. *China Business Review.* May.

"Main Tasks of Economic Construction and Reform in the First Twenty Years of the New Century." 2002. *China Daily.* December 6.

Mallon, Glenda, and John Whalley. 2004. "China's Post Accession WTO Stance." NBER Working Paper 10649. National Bureau of Economic Research, Cambridge, MA.

Mao, Xianqiang, Xiurui Guo, Yongguan Chang, and Yingdeng Peng. 2005. "Improving Air Quality in Large Cities by Substituting Natural Gas for Coal in China: Changing Idea and Incentive Policy Implications." *Energy Policy* 33 (3): 307–18.

McKibbin, Warwick J., and Wing Thye Woo. 2003. "The Consequences of China's WTO Accession on Its Neighbors." Working Paper. Australian National University, Canberra.

McKinsey Global Institute. 2001. "US Productivity Growth, 1995–2000, Section VI: Retail Trade." n.p.: McKinsey Global Institute.

Meng, Qingyue, Ling Li, and Karen Eggleston. 2004. "Health Service Delivery in China: A Critical Review." Working Paper. World Bank, Washington, DC.

Meng, Qingyue, Xingzhu Liu, and Junshi Shi. 2000. "Comparing the Services and Quality of Private and Public Clinics in Rural China." *Health Policy and Planning* 15 (4, December): 349–56.

Ministry of Public Health (China). 2001. *Chinese Health Statistical Digest*, Beijing: Chinese Ministry of Public Health (in Chinese).

Modigliani, Franco, and Shi Larry Cao. 2004. "The Chinese Saving Puzzle and the Life-Cycle Hypothesis." *Journal of Economic Literature* 42 (1): 145–70.

Mohan, T. T. Ram. 2004. "Privatisation in China: Softly, Softy Does It." *Economic and Political Weekly*. November.

Morisset, Jacques. 2003. "Tax Incentives." Private Sector and Infrastructure Network Note. World Bank, Washington, DC.

Murphey, Rhoads. 1980. *The Fading of the Maoist Vision*. New York: Methuen.

Murphy, David. 2004. "A Fearsome Thirst: China Could Solve Its Acute Water Shortage by Importing More Food Grains but That Could Leave It Vulnerable." *Far Eastern Economic Review*. July 22.

Murphy, Rachel. 2002. *How Migrant Labor Is Changing Rural China*. Cambridge, U.K.: Cambridge University Press.

Myers, Norman, and Jennifer Kent. 2004. *The New Consumers*. Washington, DC: Island Press.

Nabeshima, Kaoru. 2004. "Technology Transfer in East Asia: A Survey." In Shahid Yusuf, M. Anjum Altaf, and Kaoru Nabeshima, eds., *Global Production Networking and Technological Change in East Asia*. New York: Oxford University Press.

National Bureau of Statistics of China. Various years. *China Statistical Abstract*. Beijing: China Statistical Publishing House.

———. Various years. *China Statistical Yearbook*. Beijing: China Statistical Publishing House.

National Bureau of Statistics of China, Ministry of Labor and Social Security, Ministry of Agriculture, and All-China Federation of Trade Unions, comps. 2004. *China Labour Statistical Yearbook 2004*. Beijing: China Statistical Press.

National Bureau of Statistics of China and Ministry of Science and Technology, comps. 2002. *2001 China Statistical Yearbook on Science and Technology*. Beijing: China Statistical Press.

———, comps. 2003. *2002 China Statistical Yearbook on Science and Technology*. Beijing: China Statistical Press.

"The Net's Second Superpower." 2004. *Business Week*. March 15.

Ng, Linda F. Y., and Chyau Tuan. 2003. "Location Decisions of Manufacturing FDI in China: Implications of China's WTO Accession." *Journal of Asian Economics* 14 (1): 51–72.

Nolan, Peter. 2002. "China and the Global Business Revolution." *Cambridge Journal of Economics* 26 (1): 119–37.

———. 2004. *China at the Crossroads*. Cambridge, U.K.: Policy Press.

Nolan, Peter, Alan Shipman, and Huaichuan Rui. 2004. "Coal Liquefaction, Shenhua Group, and China's Energy Security." *European Management Journal* 22 (2): 150–64.

OECD (Organisation for Economic Co-operation and Development). 2000. *Education at a Glance: OECD Indicators.* Paris: OECD.

———. 2004a. *Patents and Innovation: Trends and Policy Challenges.* Paris: OECD.

———. 2004b. *Understanding Economic Growth.* Paris: OECD.

———. 2005a. *Main Science and Technology Indicators 2005.* Paris: OECD.

———. 2005b. *OECD Economic Surveys: China.* Paris: OECD.

"Official Misusing Education Funds Fired." 2004. *China Daily.* July 2.

"Oil and Politics Fuel Closer Ties." 2004. *Oxford Analytica.* November 18.

"Oily Diplomacy." 2006. *Business China.* January 2.

"Over a Barrel." 2004. *Lloyd's Shipping Economist.* March.

Pangestu, Mari, and Sudarshan Gooptu. 2004. "New Regionalism: Options for China and East Asia." In Kathie Krumm and Homi Kharas, eds., *East Asia Integrates.* Washington, DC: World Bank.

Park, Albert. 2004. "Rural-Urban Inequality in China." Prepared for the Eleventh Five-Year Plan of China. World Bank, Washington, DC.

Park, Albert, Sangui Wang, and Guobao Wu. 2002. "Regional Poverty Targeting in China." *Journal of Public Economics* 86 (1): 123–53.

Parker, David, and Colin Kirkpatrick. 2005. "Privatisation in Developing Countries: A Review of the Evidence and the Policy Lessons." *Journal of Development Studies* 41 (4): 513–41.

Peng, Chaoyang, Xiaodong Wu, Gordon Liu, Todd Johnson, Jitendra Shah, and Sarath Guttikunda. 2002. "Urban Air Quality and Health in China." *Urban Studies* 39 (12): 2283–99.

"People-Centered Development Gains Ground." 2004. *Oxford Analytica.* November 26.

Perkins, Dwight H. 2004. "Corporate Governance, Industrial Policy, and the Rule of Law." In Shahid Yusuf, M. Anjum Altaf, and Kaoru Nabeshima, eds., *Global Change and East Asian Policy Initiatives.* Washington, DC: World Bank and New York: Oxford University Press.

Pingali, P. L., ed. 2001. *CIMMYT 1999–2000 World Maize Facts and Trends: Meeting World Maize Needs: Technological Opportunities and Priorities for the Public Sector.* Mexico, DF: International Maize and Wheat Improvement Center (CIMMYT).

"Pollution Costing Shanghai." 2005. *China Business Review.* November.

"Power Shortage Sees China Target Big Energy Users." 2004. *Japan Times.* July 8.

Pritchett, Lant. 2004. "The Lack of Education." In Bjorn Lomborg, eds., *Global Crises, Global Solutions.* Cambridge, U.K.: Cambridge University Press.

"Province Achieves Rapid Growth." 2004. *China Daily*. October 26.

Putterman, Louis, and Xiao-yuan Dong. 2000. "China's State-Owned Enterprises." *Modern China* 26 (4): 403–47.

Qiu, Haiying. 2001. "Nongcun Laodongli Huiliu Yu Laodongli Miji Xing Changye Di Kaifa [Return Labor Migration and the Development of Labor-Intensive Industry]." *Renkou Xuekan [Population Journal]*) 3: 52–55.

"The Quest for Energy to Grow." 2002. *Far Eastern Economic Review*. June 20.

Rappaport, Jordan, and Jeffrey D. Sachs. 2003. "The United States as a Coastal Nation." *Journal of Economic Growth* 8 (1): 5–46.

Ravallion, Martin. 2004. "Pro-Poor Growth: A Primer." World Bank, Washington, DC.

Ravallion, Martin, and Shaohua Chen. 2004. "China's (Uneven) Progress against Poverty." World Bank, Washington, DC.

Riskin, Carl. 1987. *China's Political Economy*. New York: Oxford University Press.

Rong, Zhao, and Yang Yao. 2003. "Public Service Provision and the Demand for Electric Appliances in Rural China." *China Economic Review* 14 (2): 131–41.

Rosen, Daniel H., Scott Rozelle, and Jikun Huang. 2004. *Roots of Competitiveness: China's Evolving Agriculture Interests*. Washington, DC: Institute for International Economics.

Rosenthal, Stuart S., and William C. Strange. 2003. "Evidence on the Nature and Sources of Agglomeration Economics." Mimeo. Center for Policy Reserach, Syracuse University; Rotman School of Management, University of Toronto.

Rumbaugh, Thomas, and Nicolas Blancher. 2003. "China: International Trade and WTO Accession." IMF Working Paper WP/03/245. International Monetary Fund, Washington, DC.

Sachs, Jeffrey D., and Wing Thye Woo. 1997. *Understanding China's Economic Performance*. Development Discussion Paper 575. Cambridge, MA: Harvard Institute for International Development.

Saggi, Kamal. 2002. "Trade, Foreign Direct Investment, and International Technology Transfer: A Survey." *World Bank Research Observer* 17 (2): 191–235.

Saha, Biswatosh. 2004. "State Support for Industrial R and D in Developing Economies." *Economic and Political Weekly*. August 28.

Saich, Anthony. 2004. "The Changing Role of Government." Paper prepared for the Report on China's Eleventh Five-Year Plan. World Bank, Washington, DC.

Sakakibara, Eisuke, and Sharon Yamakawa. 2004. "Trade and Foreign Direct Investment: A Role for Regionalism." In Shahid Yusuf, M. Anjum Altaf, and Kaoru Nabeshima, eds., *Global Change and East Asian Policy Initiatives*. New York: Oxford University Press.

"Satellite View Alerts China to Soaring Pollution." 2005. *Nature* 437 (12, September): 12.

Schultz, T. Paul. 2004. "Access to Education: Alternative Perspective." In Bjorn Lomborg, ed., *Global Crises, Global Solutions.* Cambridge, U.K.: Cambridge University Press.

Scott, Allen J. 2001. "Globalization and the Rise of City-Regions." *European Planning Studies* 9 (7): 813–26.

Scott, Allen J., and Michael Storper. 2003. "Regions, Globalization, Development." *Regional Studies* 37 (6-7): 579–93.

SEPA (State Environmental Protection Administration). 2003. *Report on the State of the Environment in China* 2002. Beijing: SEPA.

Shafaeddin, S. M. 2002. *The Impact of China's Accession to WTO on the Exports of Developing Countries.* UNCTAD Discussion Paper 160. Geneva, Switzerland: United Nations Conference on Trade and Development.

Shalizi, Zmarak. 2004. "Water Issues and Options in China." Prepared for the Eleventh Five-Year Plan of China. World Bank, Washington, DC.

Shanghai Municipal Statistical Bureau. 2005. *Shanghai Statistical Yearbook 2005.* Beijing: China Statistical Bureau.

Shine, Kenneth I. 2004. "Technology and Health." *Technology in Society* 26 (2-3): 137–48.

Smarzynska Javorcik, Beata. 2004. "The Composition of Foreign Direct Investment and Protection of Intellectual Property Rights: Evidence from Transition Economies." *European Economic Review* 48 (1): 39–62.

Smil, Vaclav 1984. *The Bad Earth: Environmental Degradation in China.* New York: M. E. Sharpe.

———. 2002. "Energy Resources and Uses: A Global Primer for the Twenty-First Century." *Current History* 101 (653): 126–32.

———. 2004. *China's Past, China's Future.* New York: Routledge.

———. 2005. "China's Thirsty Future." *Far Eastern Economic Review* (December): 29–33.

Smith, Peter, Christine Wong, and Yuxin Zhao. 2004. "Public Expenditure and Resource Allocation in the Health Sector in China." Working Paper. World Bank, Washington, DC.

Smyth, Russell, Jianguo Wang, and Quek Lee Kiang. 2002. "Efficiency, Performance, and Changing Corporate Governance in China's Township-Village Enterprises since the 1990s." *Asia Pacific Economic Literature* 15 (1): 30–41.

Solomon, Barry D. and Abhijit Banerjee. 2006. "A Global Survey of Hydrogen Energy Research, Development and Policy." *Energy Policy* 34 (7): 781–792.

Solow, Robert M. 2001. "NCN Summit 2001: Information Technology and the Recent Productivity Boom in the US." http://web.mit.edu/cmi-videos/solow/text.html.

"Something in the Air." 2006. *New Scientist*. January 21.

"South-East Asia: China Boom Puts Shipping Under Stress" 2004. *Oxford Analytica*. September 22.

"State Intellectual Property Office of China." 2005. http://www.sipo.gov.cn/ sipo_English/ndbg/nb/ndbg2004/default.htm.

Steinfeld, Edward. 2004a. "China's Shallow Integration: Networked Production and the New Challenges for Late Industrialization." *World Development*. 32 (11): 1971–1987.

Steinfeld, Edward. 2004b. 'Energy Policy: Charting a Path for China's Future." Paper prepared for the Report on Eleventh Five-Year Plan. World Bank, Washington, DC.

"Step by Step." 2004. The *Economist*. September 2.

Storper, Michael, and Anthony J. Venables. 2002. "Buzz: The Economic Force of the City." Presented at DRUID Summer Conference on "Industrial Dynamics of the New and Old Economy: Who Is Embracing Whom?" Copenhagen, June 6.

Sun, Yifei. 2002. "China's National Innovation System in Transition." *Eurasian Geography and Economics* 43 (6): 476–92.

Tan, Kong-Yam. 2004. "Market Fragmentation and Impact on Economics Growth." Prepared for the Eleventh Five-Year Plan of China. World Bank, Washington, DC.

Tanner, Murray Scot. 2004. "China Rethinks Unrest." *The Washington Quarterly* 27 (3): 137–56.

Taylor, John. 2004a. "Contemporary China: Poverty, Vulnerability, and Social Cohesion." Paper prepared for the Report on Eleventh Five-Year Plan. World Bank, Washington, DC.

Taylor, John J. 2004b. "The Nuclear Power Bargain." *Issues in Science and Technology Online* (Spring). http://www.issues.org/20.3/taylor.html.

Temple, Jonathan. 1999. "The New Growth Evidence." *Journal of Economic Literature* 37 (1): 112–56.

"Too Fast in China?" 2006. *Washington Post*. January 26.

"Trade Surpluses Set to Grow." 2005. *Oxford Analytica*. July 26.

"Tyre Industry Hit by Explosion in Demand." 2004. *Financial Times*. December 3.

UNCTAD (United Nations Conference on Trade and Development). 2005. *Trade and Development Report, 2005*. New York: United Nations.

UNDP (United Nations Development Programme). 2004. *Establishing a Xiao Kang Society*. New York: United Nations.

———. 2005. *China Human Development Report 2005*. New York: United Nations.

"An Unquenchable Thirst." 2004. The *Economist*. June 19.

"UN Reports Upsurge in FDI to Developing Countries." 2005. *Financial Times.* January 11.

Wang, Hong. 2005. "China's Fragmented Health-System Reforms." *Lancet* 366 (October): 1257–58.

Wang, Sangui, Zhou Li, and Yanshun Ren. 2003. "The 8-7 National Poverty Reduction Program in China: the National Strategy and Its Impact." Mimeo. World Bank, Washington, DC.

Wang, Yan. 2002. "China: Inequality in Education and Health Outcomes." Background paper for the China 2002 Country Economic Memorandum. World Bank, Washington, DC.

———. 2004. "China: Inequalities in Education and Health Outcomes." World Bank, Washington, DC.

"Water Rate Hikes Stayed for Now." 2004. *China Daily.* July 2.

Watts, Jonathan. 2005. "China: The Air Pollution Capital of the World." *Lancet* 366 (November): 1761–62.

Wei, Yehia Dennis, and Wangming Li. 2002. "Reforms, Globalization, and Urban Growth in China." *Eurasian Geography and Economics* 43 (6): 459–75.

Weist, Dana. 2004. "Issues in Rural Finance and Service Delivery." Paper prepared for the Report on China's Eleventh Five-Year Plan. World Bank, Washington, DC.

Wells, Luis T. Jr., Nancy J. Allen, Jacques Morisset, and Neda Pirnia. 2001. *Using Tax Incentives to Compete for Foreign Investment: Are They Worth the Costs?* FIAS Occasional Paper 15. Washington, DC: International Finance Corporation.

Wen, Jiabao. 2004. *Report of the World of the Government.* n.p.: n.p.

Wen, Mei. 2004. "Bankruptcy, Sale, and Mergers as a Route to the Reform of Chinese SOEs." *China Economic Review* 15 (3): 249–67.

"West-East Gas Pipeline Link Nears Completion" 2004a. *China Daily.* August 30.

"West-East Gas Pipeline Starts Full Operation." 2004b. *China Daily.* October 1.

Whalley, John. 2003. "Liberalization in China's Key Service Sectors Following WTO Accession: Some Scenarios and Issues of Measurement." NBER Working Paper 10143. National Bureau of Economic Research, Cambridge, MA.

Whalley, John, and Shunming Zhang. 2004. "Inequality Change in China and (Hukou) Labor Mobility Restrictions." NBER Working Paper 10683. National Bureau of Economic Research, Cambridge, MA.

"What Goes Up..." 2006. *Business China.* January 2.

Wieser, Robert. 2005. "Research and Development Productivity and Spillovers: Empirical Evidence at the Firm Level." *Journal of Economic Surveys* 19 (4): 587–621.

Woetzel, Jonathan R. 2003. *Capitalist China: Strategies for a Revolutionized Economy.* Singapore: John Wiley and Sons (Asia).

World Bank. 2001a. "Agenda for Water Sector Strategy for North China." World Bank, Washington, DC.

———. 2001b. *China: Air, Land, and Water.* Washington, DC: World Bank.

———. 2002a. "China: Agenda for Water Sector Strategy for North China; Summary Report." World Bank, Washington, DC.

———. 2002b. *China: National Development and Sub-national Finance: A Review of Provincial Expenditures.* Report 22951-CHA. Washington, DC: World Bank.

———. 2002c. *World Development Report 2003.* Washington, DC: World Bank.

———. 2003a. "China: Promoting Growth with Equity." Report 24169-CHA. Country Economic Memorandum. World Bank, Washington, DC.

———. 2003b. *Global Economic Prospects 2004.* Washington, DC: World Bank.

———. 2003c. "Public Finance Reform and Macroeconomic Management." World Bank Policy Note. World Bank, Washington, DC.

———. 2003d. "Reform of Social Protection Mechanisms." World Bank Policy Note. World Bank, Washington, DC.

———. 2004a. "China Poor Rural Communities Development Project." Report Project Appraisal Document PO71094. World Bank, Washington, DC.

———. 2004b. "China: Food Security Brief." World Bank, Washington, DC.

———. 2004c. "Energy Sector Brief." World Bank, Washington, DC.

———. 2004d. "Regional Overview (April 2004)." World Bank, East Asia Unit, Washington, DC.

———. 2004e. *World Development Indicators.* Washington, DC: World Bank.

———. 2005a. "China's Rising Inequality and Its Income Distribution System." Mimeo. World Bank, Beijing.

———. 2005b. "East Asia Update (November 2005)." World Bank, East Asia Unit, Washington, DC.

———. 2005c. *World Development Indicators.* Washington, DC: World Bank.

"World Is Dancing to a Chinese Tune." 2004. *Financial Times.* December 7.

"World Reserves of Oil, Gas in Good Shape." 2004. *China Daily.* July 1.

Wu, Libo, Shinji Kaneko, and Shunji Matsuoka. 2005. "Driving Forces behind the Stagnancy of China's Energy-Related CO_2 Emissions from 1996 to 1999: The Relative Importance of Structural Change, Intensity Change, and Scale Change." *Energy Policy* 33 (3): 319–35.

Wu, Ziping, Minquan Liu, and John Davis. 2005. "Land Consolidation and Productivity in Chinese Household Crop Production." *China Economic Review* 16 (1): 28–49.

Yang, Dennis Tao. 1997. "China's Land Arrangements and Rural Labor Mobility." *China Economic Review* 8 (2): 101–16.

Yang, Hongxing, John Burnett, and Qingyuan Zhang. 2001. "Renewable Energy Applications and Impacts on Greenhouse Gas Emission in China." *World Resource Review* 13 (1): 123.

Yang, Yongzheng. 2003. "China's Integration into the World Economy: Implications for Developing Countries." IMF Working Paper WP/03/245. International Monetary Fund, Washington, DC.

Yao, Shujie. 2002. "China's Rural Economy in the First Decade of the Twenty-first Century: Problems and Growth Constraints." *China Economic Review* 13 (4): 354–60.

Yusuf, Shahid, M. Anjum Altaf, Barry Eichengreen, Sudarshan Gooptu, Kaoru Nabeshima, Charles Kenny, Dwight H. Perkins, and Marc Shotten. 2003. *Innovative East Asia: The Future of Growth.* New York: Oxford University Press.

Yusuf, Shahid, and Simon J. Evenett. 2002. *Can East Asia Compete? Innovation for Global Markets.* New York: Oxford University Press.

Yusuf, Shahid, and Kaoru Nabeshima. 2005. "Creative Industries in East Asia." *Cities* 22 (2): 109–22.

———. 2006. "Two Decades of Reform: The Changing Organization Dynamics of Chinese Industrial Firms." Policy Research Working Paper. World Bank, Washington, DC.

Yusuf, Shahid, Kaoru Nabeshima, and Dwight H. Perkins. 2005. *Under New Ownership: Privatizing China's State-Owned Enterprises.* Palo Alto, CA: Stanford University Press.

Yusuf, Shahid, Shuilin Wang, and Kaoru Nabeshima. 2005. "Fiscal Policies for Innovation." World Bank, Washington, DC.

Zhang, Kevin Honglin, and Shunfeng Song. 2001. "Promoting Exports: The Role of Inward FDI in China." *China Economic Review* 11 (4): 385–96.

Zhang, Le-Yin. 2004. "The Role of Corporatization and Stock Market Listing in Reforming China's State Industry." *World Development* 32 (12): 2031–47.

Zhang, Li. 2001. *Strangers in the City: Reconfigurations of Space, Power, and Social Networks within China's Floating Population.* Palo Alto, CA: Stanford University Press.

Zhang, Linxiu, Jikun Huang, and Scott Rozelle. 2002. "Employment, Emerging Labor Markets, and the Role of Education in Rural China." *China Economic Review* 13 (4): 313–28.

Zhang, Ping, and Zi Lin. 2000. "Market Economic Development and Reform of Household Registration System in China." *Population and Economics* 6: 35–41.

Zhang, Qing, and Bruce Felmingham. 2001. "The Relationship between Inward Direct Foreign Investment and China's Provincial Export Trade." *China Economic Review* 12 (1): 82–99.

Zhang, Zhong Xiang. 2003. "Why Did the Energy Intensity Fall in China's Industrial Sector in the 1990's? The Relative Importance of Structural Change and Intensity Change." *Energy Economics* 25 (6): 625–38.

Zhao, Jimin, and Marc W. Malaina. 2006. "Transition to Hydrogen-Based Transportation in China: Lessons Learned from Alternative Fuel Vehicle Programs in the United States and China." *Energy Policy* 34 (11): 1299–1309.

Zhao, Min. 2005. "Policies for the Eleventh Foreign Capital Utilization Plan." Mimeo. World Bank, Beijing.

Zhao, Zong-Ci, and Ying Xu. 2002. "Detection and Scenarios of Temperature Change in East Asia." *World Resource Review* 14 (3): 321–33.

Zhu, Jieming. 2004. "From Land Use Right to Land Development Right: Institutional Change in China's Urban Development." *Urban Studies* 41 (7): 1249–67.

———. 2005. "A Transitional Institution for the Emerging Land Market in Urban China." *Urban Studies* 42 (8): 1369–90.

Zittel, Werner, and Manfred Treber. 2004. "Analysis of BP Statistical Review of World Energy with Respect to CO2 Emissions (5th Edition)." Briefing Paper. Germanwatch, Bonn, Germany.

Index